**MAY 5**

Yesterday was the 1st Day of the rest of my life!!!

Got skater pants. Went to the communion. Was a hit!

No more Miss Nice Girl. Look out world.

# *Fine Fine Music*

STORIES BY

CASSIE J. SNEIDER

● Bunk Bed Press ●
Oakland, California

Previously Published:
"Mole" and "One More Saturday Night" in *the2ndhand*
"A Woman Soon" in Sadie Magazine


ALL NAMES IN THE BOOK CHANGED EXCEPT FOR
THOSE WHO GAVE THEIR LOVING APPROVAL.


Copyright © Cassie J. Sneider 2012

All rights reserved, especially the right to party.

No part of this book may be reproduced or transmitted in
any form or by any means, written, electronic, or mechanical
(unless for review purposes), except with written permission
by the author. Don't be a jerk about it.

ISBN: 978-0-9850385-0-2

Cover Drawings: Cassie J. Sneider
Cover Layout: Ric Carrasquillo (www.squillostudio.com)
Author Photo, Cover Photo: Evan Felts (www.evanfelts.com)

Content photos courtesy of the Sneider family archive.

Printed on 100% recycled pcw, acid free paper
in California, USA by 1984 Printing,
www.1984printing.com

This book is for my dad, and also for Dave.

★

"I think I saw you in an ice cream parlor,
drinking milkshakes cold and long.
Smiling and waving and looking so fine,
don't think you knew you were in this song."

- David Bowie

# STORIES

## *One More Saturday Night*

In the bathroom at work, my gaze jumps between a thirty-year-old promotional poster of Sha Na Na and my feet swinging just above the piss-encrusted floor. I am the only woman to break the gender barrier at the record store in its thirty-four year history and the bathroom is gross. A black mold has formed in the sink from a drip that has been active for a generation. Pieces of wet toilet paper have mummified onto the dark wood paneling and the mirror has turned orange between the glass and metallic coating, giving reflections a haunted, otherworldly appearance. I have cleaned this bathroom twice in my career here and both times were when a coworker left feces on the seat, which lingered for four days until I gave in and sprayed it down, gagging and wearing latex gloves.

I try to stay hydrated on the job. Adding "thirsty" to the mix of "generally irritable" and "never sleeps" doesn't make for a positive workday experience. I get hit on by middle-aged men all day, and if I were not in constant supply of bottled water, my title of Smiling, Cleverly Rude Tattooed Girl would be traded in favor of Openly Hostile, Dehydrated, Alternative-Looking Bitch. As much as I hate my town, I enjoy the novelty of being Ronkonkoma's [1] sweetheart and do not wish to jeopardize it. I bring five bottles of water to work and usually visit Sha Na Na about six or seven times a shift.

The poster is an unusual choice of decor for a store populated by men. Sha Na Na is taped to the bathroom door,

---

[1] The name of my hometown is pronounced "Ron-Kahn-Kuh-Muh." Christina Ricci mentions it in the movie 200 Cigarettes, but does a poor job reproducing the accent. If I were to recast that movie using regular customers at the record store, I would take on her role, and the Casey Affleck character would be played by the guy who came in every day to ask if Hatebreed put out a new album on the way to his job corralling the carts at the grocery store.

opposite where someone has graffiti'd, BEATLES TOURS 1966-PRESENT=0. Sha Na Na is posed in varied stages of greaser cool, perched on trashcans in an alley, running combs through their hair, sneering or looking indifferent to the lens. They are wearing leather jackets and pedal pushers, cut-off denim vests and muscle shirts, ostentatiously flexing for the camera. Sha Na Na is young, beautiful and tormented. Sha Na Na fucks on the first date. The skyscrapers rise up over Sha Na Na, laundry lines strewn from fire escape to fire escape, but the urban landscape doesn't get Sha Na Na down. They own everything this side of the tracks.

The Long Island Railroad cuts Ronkonkoma in half, which I always hoped would mean I lived on the wrong side of the tracks. Although my side has a haunted lake and a trailer park, the other side is home to an industrial park with a strip club called "Sugar Bush." That side has an airport, boarded-up buildings, and vacant lots. This side has a retirement home, a candy shop, and the record store, making it less seedy than my imagination wishes it was. There are many bars in Ronkonkoma and an equal number of Camaros swerving between them at all times of the day. Kids skateboard in the bank parking lot. Geriatrics motor along on Rascals and carry heavy gallons of milk like they are sandbags. Ronkonkoma is populated with lawns of crabgrass and no sidewalks, but it is an altogether okay neighborhood.

I feel like I really get Sha Na Na. Not just for the obvious reason that they are the image I wish to cultivate for myself, but because they were *of the wrong time.* Sha Na Na missed the West Side Story-boat by twenty years. They doo-wopped Top 40 radio of the seventies right over the head, blindsiding the disco movement with sweet harmonies and antiquated hand jives. I work in a record store in the twenty-first century. I help people who can't afford iPods or aftermarket stereos dig through the cassettes to find Saigon Kick and Tesla tapes.

I hear a lot of great stories of how things used to be. All-night parties, midnight releases, boozing in the store. Home of the bootleg LP. Any live show you could want. In-store performances. Young people with mohawks working the counter in yellowed pictures. Ramones shirts. Plaid jackets. Nothing but vinyl. The New York Dolls played around the corner, you know. Ronkonkoma: 180 grams of balls and possibility, breathing down the neck of Long Island, daring you to start something. *Go ahead.*

"How about the guy with the moustache? Real quiet?" Alvin said. It was morning and we were talking about regulars at the store. I didn't know him. "Wears flannel? Comes in every Saturday ten minutes before closing. Won't leave and doesn't buy anything?

"Oh! That guy!"

"Yeah, that guy!" We stood nodding in a moment of mutual recognition. We both knew that guy.

"Yeah, I hate that guy," he said.

I had never noticed That Guy didn't buy anything, or that he lingered after closing on Saturdays. I thought I knew every regular customer, their likes and dislikes, the offish characteristics that come from staying in one place for a whole lifetime. Technically, as Tattoo Girl From the Record Store, I was no different than they were. I was a bookmark, keeping a page on the main drag of town for people with bleachy perms and acid-washed jeans. I fit in somewhere between cashing a check and losing it at The Dirty Martini.

"I never really noticed," I said.

"Yeah. Can't stand him," Alvin said. "I tell him I'm closing. He stays twenty more minutes and says he'll come back on Tuesday to buy stuff. He never comes back, and he never buys anything."

I shook my head in disapproval, but inside I felt like I had let That Guy down in not noticing him. Part of the psychology of being a regular anywhere is that you have both an identifiable characteristic and specific time frame in which you exist. This person had both, and I had failed him. I vowed to take note the next time.

Alvin left, and I loafed through the rest of the day. I was on two hours of sleep, which used to cut it until the onset of my mid-twenties. I didn't even drink coffee then, but managed to stay alert for twenty hours a day. I was on edge all the time, but it never occurred to me to sleep.

"Sleep is for the weak! I've got better things to do!" was my mantra. My logic was that while the world was sleeping, I was maintaining a higher productivity rate than everyone else. This gave me the upper hand over the somnambulistic public whose bodies were repairing themselves by processing memories and making white blood cells while I was sewing handbags and making tapes. As a result, I cannot remember anything that happened from the ages of nineteen until twenty-four. I don't think I should be held accountable for my actions during those years, but that is like an alcoholic parent asking his cigar-burned children for amnesty. Sorry, guys.

There were a lot of regulars at the jobs I had back then, but I am sure I only noticed half of them as I stumbled around in a tweaker's insomnia. At the record store, I notice everyone. The irregular stitching on their jeans. The strange urine smells. If it's tar or asphalt or concrete spotting their steel-toed boots. What union logo adorns the pockets of their shirts. The memories they share with me because I am friendly and they have no one else to talk to.

"I bet you've never even *heard* of Motorhead!" Or Hot Tuna. Or Foreigner. Or Steve Winwood. Or any other artist that came out before the turn of the century. "Saw them at the Commack Arena in '78. Quiet Riot opened. Fuck, that was a long time ago. How old are you? Eighteen? Yeah. I remember that age. *Shit, that was a good show.*"

No one seems to notice that I am not eighteen, that I have bags under my eyes and enough body modifications to indicate that I am probably not a teenager, but a displaced Aborigine. I nod, taking their memory and tucking it away in my brain where it will one day replace long division or my mother's birthday. Each story that slips out when someone spies the first record they ever bought or rolls through town for the first time in twenty years to ask if the same guy still owns the place settles somewhere in my brain like the snow in a souvenir globe. I listen, sometimes irritated, sometimes intently, drinking my coffee and wondering how they ended up here, spilling their memories on long-play to a total stranger.

I am flossing my teeth in the orange bathroom mirror, thinking about Sha Na Na. We were both placed here accidentally on purpose by something beyond our control. They gaze at me while I floss, saying, *"Aaaay! You're gonna miss this place!"* and, *"Rock and roll is here to stay!"*

I hear someone enter the store and toss the floss. It's ten to seven and That Guy is here to check out records.

"Hey, man," I say, playing it cool. "Ten minutes."

He nods. We are there until 7:20, but I do not get angry. We both have our parts to play. Mine is to drink enough liquids, narrate everything in my head, and listen.

"Are these bootlegs pressed or burned?"

"Can you get Van Halen at the Coliseum in 1980?"

"Is it soundboard?"

"That was such a good show."

"I had fourth row. Went with my best friend."

"Haven't seen him in twenty years."

"Heard you say on the phone you only got three hours sleep."

"You gotta get home and sleep, so I'll come back Tuesday."

"See ya."

His car is filled with trash. Bags and clothes. He drives away and I turn out the light. I count the drawer and set the alarm. Then I walk to my car and drive to the all-night diner on the other side of the Ronkonkoma train tracks.

"Isn't it a little early for you?" the night manager says in his Greek accent.

"I just got out of work," says The Girl with Tattoos and Laptop, settling into her usual booth. She orders black coffee and one slice of cheesecake, nursing them until she is done pecking out a story, leaving a five-dollar tip and making small talk with the waiters, busboys, and anyone else who will talk to her. She goes home, crossing over the tracks again, passing the bars, and the people, and the neon lights advertising COMPACT DISCS, LPS, TAPES BOUGHT AND SOLD, and thinks about how the timing is always all wrong.

# *Sweet Emotion*

What is it about *guitars*?

What is it about guitars that makes every fifteen year-old crave the feel of metal and sound springing from their fingertips; the magic quality that makes you a hundred times cooler once the first chord is struck; that once you're holding one, you are Elvis on *Ed Sullivan,* Johnny Cash flipping off the BBC or Hendrix conjuring flame?

When I was fifteen, I fell passionately, pathetically in love with Donny, the son of my mother's friend. I only saw him once a year at an annual barbecue, which made the logistics of this crush impossible. That summer, I noticed Donny had turned from a shy boy with a collection of pet turtles into a spiky-haired, ball-chain-necklace-wearing, Slayer-shirted disciple of rock and roll. Donny was now a sex object, whereas I had only just started to wake from my coma of awkwardness. That very day, on a school-shopping excursion, I protested the shoes my mother picked out for me. For some reason, each year, my sister and I were outfitted in a brand of sneakers called Balloons, which had Velcro closures and a thick but lightweight orthopedic sole, perfect for running from girls with crimpy hair who follow you off the bus and want to kick your ass for no reason at all. I'm certain that my mother received a secret kickback from this company, because we had to search far and wide to find these obscure, hideous sneakers.

I had an older cousin who skateboarded and threw *Oh-Shit-It's-the-Cops* parties when her parents left for the weekend. Lenore wore Vans and she seemed to be faring well in high school. Her success led me to believe that if I had Vans, I could be one step closer to Maximum Popularity, the definitive goal of being fifteen. That day, I thwarted my mother's best efforts and walked away from the department store with a puke-green pair of Vans, which she warned me were "boy shoes" and by wearing them, everyone would think I was a boy. In my mother's eyes, I might as well have been main-lining testosterone, but it was a chance I was willing to take. There are always side effects to changing your identity.

The rest of my wardrobe was a horrific amalgamation of poor kid hand-me-downs. The day of the barbecue I had carefully selected an outfit that might allow me to be accepted by members of my peer group. I chose a button-down Dave Coulier-style shirt I had stolen from my stepdad. It was patterned with gray geometric shapes and, months later, thrown out by my mother for its ugliness, which she still will not admit to today. I wore my coolest pair of cut-off shorts, which I had boldly embroidered "U2" in orange on the ass for maximum street cred. I had a chubby face, swollen with salt from the TV dinners we ate every night, and a frizzy, shoulder-length, Charles Manson haircut that hung in my eyes for extra mystery.

I was unfuckable in every conceivable way.

I watched Donny out of the corner of my eye, stuffing my mouth with fruit salad in self-conscious reflex while someone told the story of the time my mother knocked somebody out with a chair in a bar fight before I was born. Donny wore his angst in a cheerful, self-assured manner. I had never seen a boy look so cool. Sure, Mean People Sucked as the patch on his calf-length shorts said, but he brooded with positivity.

Donny looked at me from across the table. "Hey, this sucks. Wanna hang out with me and my friends?"

No boy had ever talked to me except to copy my homework because I wore glasses and looked studious by default. And certainly no boy had ever willingly thrown an invitation to hang out in my busted direction.

My voice came out in a rasp, choked by nerves and a hunk of watermelon.

"*Yes!*"

Donny, me, and two of his friends walked to an overpass where they talked about "hardcore," something I had never heard of. It sounded forbidden, like it could be found on Cinemax late at night. *Overthrow. Destroyed by Anger. Indecision.* I had no idea what they were talking about, but the words sounded like the angry clattering of horseshoes, something frenetic and dissonant, the type of thing that made parents silent at holiday dinners just knowing you'd participated in it.

"What do you listen to?" they asked.

"Reel Big Fish. Save Ferris. The Mighty Mighty Bosstones." My musical radar skanked to the frequencies of radio ska. Band names steeped in plays-on-words and oddball generational movie references. I omitted Aerosmith, aware enough to know that would incur judgment.

*I suck in every imaginable way,* I thought, hoping this wouldn't inspire them to "overthrow" me off the overpass because I had bad taste.

"That's cool. I've got *Turn the Radio Off,*" Donny said, and I was relieved. After a while, we walked back to his house. My mom was sitting on Donny's mom's lap and my stepdad had accidentally cut his finger on a bottle. Everything was so embarrassing, and I turned six shades of red under my wooly serial killer hair, smiling in spite of myself. Donny and his friends seemed to genuinely enjoy my company. I was saying humorous, worthwhile things instead of going into a socially-induced anaphylactic shock. Maybe I didn't suck so much.

"Let's jam," one of his friends said. As a unit, they walked to the guitar cases and drum set I hadn't noticed lying next to a wall. They plugged in and wailed for an hour. I watched every chord, struck grateful for the first time in my teenage life while my parents drank coffee under citronella torches, reanimating the best years of their lives in sloshed words and slurry gestures.

"Hey," Donny said, taking the strap from around his neck. "Wanna play?" He handed me the guitar, an unclassifiable black and white number. It could have been John Lennon's Les Paul, or it could have been from Wal-Mart. I didn't know anything about guitars. But I did know how I imagined I would look if I were holding one as I strummed a broken pool cue in the mirror to *Toys in the Attic* each day. The crowd went wild. I was a star.

I never thought I would ever be cool enough to touch a guitar. I was the first person in my family to ever try an instrument, which was a failed two- month stint of clarinet in fourth grade. Donny handed me a pick, and I strummed gently, terrified of breaking the strings.

"No, dude," he said. *"Rock it!"*

I did not play chords, but the guitar came alive in my hands. This was teenage revolution. This was rock and roll.

I asked for a guitar for my sixteenth birthday, crazed by months of thinking about that day. There was only one way to get back that feeling. In the meantime, I had learned what hardcore was. It was my sister's birthday, and Lenore and I were hiding out in my room. If I needed to know more about this subculture of Vans-wearers, I had to go straight to the source.

"What's hardcore?" I asked.

"What do you mean, 'What's hardcore?'"

"I dunno. I heard someone say it once and I thought you might know what it was."

"It's a type of music where you punch the floor and go apeshit," Lenore said, as if explaining the process of milk pasteurization or how a hip is replaced.

"How did you find out what it was?"

"You go to shows and listen to music," she said, losing patience.

"Shows?" I felt like a German exchange student.

"Where *bands* play. Clubs, bars, VFW halls. Jesus, I guess I gotta take you to a hardcore show now."

In my head, a hardcore show looked like a scene out of *Teenage Mutant Ninja Turtles: The Movie*. Kids were putting out cigarettes on their teeth and spray-painting the concrete walls of an abandoned warehouse.

"Awesome! I can't wait!"

But I did wait, because Lenore did not get around to taking me to a show for another two years. That was probably a wise decision on her part because by the time she took me to my first show, I had burst through my cocoon of awkwardness to reveal…a moth. A pale, brown-haired moth with an affinity for punk music.

My whole life, I had been an Aerosmith fan. This seems an unlikely choice of fan devotion for a female coming of age in the late nineties, but everything in my life seems to happen on a time delay similar to the movie *The Explorers*. Society will advance to flying cars and white noise as a form of music, and I'll still be listening to a cassette of *Pump,* thinking I'm treading the cutting edge. The fact that Aerosmith was my favorite band from the ages of nine to nineteen is a result of the time-released fetal alcohol syndrome I am convinced my parents gave me.

When I was nine, my stepdad rolled his Camaro in an accident. After his bones reset, he and my mother went to the tow yard to salvage objects from the car. One of the things they came back with was a bag of tapes. They were covered in sand, wet grass, and beer.

"Take what you want. They probably won't work."

It was a white-trash Christmas in July. Really? Broken tapes? For me?

I picked *Toys in the Attic* because I had an attic bedroom and could identify with the morose, forgotten toys on the cover. The tape not only worked, but it *blew my mind.* Until that point, the only tapes I had were Michael Jackson's *Bad* and the Teenage Mutant Ninja Turtles' *Coming Out of Our Shells Tour,* which cannot be considered rock, even though Splinter does have a pretty sweet power ballad.

Looking back on our relationship, I don't know if Aerosmith and I ever really understood each other. Aerosmith sang of love in elevators, not about being fourteen and having a crush on Kelvin Flag, who said "I love you" in front of your whole eighth grade French class and you thought they were laughing because you and Kelvin were perfect together. *They* were internationally recognized rock icons, and I would probably live my *whole life* without ever being fellated in a locker room under Giants Stadium. We were living in two different worlds.

When I thought about it, I realized that Aerosmith had probably never been fourteen. They had been grown in a lab, tanned, and made love to. But there was something about the hardcore and punk music I had been introduced to that was different. These songs said everything my heart and brain were crying out for, but lacked the eloquence to say. It was every unspoken word that died in my throat when I got thrown into a locker or harassed on the bus. In every song there was the hope that maybe I wasn't going to stay fourteen for the rest of my life, and I was willing to keep trying as long as they were willing to keep singing.

When I asked for a guitar, my mother offered to get me a nameplate, a name-ring, anything gold or sparkly as long as it had my name on it, because every sixteen-year-old girl should have an identifying piece of jewelry so some frat guy can know what to call her while he's putting rohypnol in her drink. I refused to have my finger sized and bought a guitar myself. I purchased it at Costco, which is not the most rock and roll place in the world, but certainly an economically sound decision. I assumed that all my years of listening to *Toys in the Attic* on repeat had made me some kind of musical prodigy. I'd always felt that I would instinctively play a wicked solo by tapping the frets with my tongue, just like Joe Perry might have done on the *Permanent Vacation* tour.

Most of my time with the actual guitar was no different than the time I'd spent in front of the mirror pretending I had one: jumping with it from couch to couch and doing Steven Tyler kicks at the mirror. And since I had used all my money buying the guitar in the first place, I couldn't afford lessons. Instead, I bought myself a how-to book on clearance, cracked my knuckles, and dove headfirst into the exciting world of trying to read music. The book I bought was pretty useless, and the only songs I ever learned were the same ones I'd learned on clarinet in the fourth grade. Before I gave up on guitar, you could hear me late at night in my room, angrily strumming an angst-ridden version of Beethoven's "Ode to Joy."

I have only seen Donny one other time in these ten years. I was sixteen and sitting in the food court of the mall with my cousins. I was wearing a green ringer T-shirt with colorful Japanese robots locked in battle. I had no idea what cartoon they were from, or that people into anime usually one day LARPed their way into no longer being able to function in society. I thought I looked pretty rock and roll, in spite of my track pants, overbite, and thick, myopic Mark David Chapman glasses. I saw him standing near the pay phones and ran over.

"Wow! It's been so long! What are you doing at *the mall?*" I asked, overwhelmed by my good fortune. I don't know what I was expecting him to say. Maybe that he'd been obsessing about me for six months, too. Maybe that he had also drawn a detailed graphic novel about the night we hung out. Maybe he would ask me to go to a Madball show and teach me how to play my newly acquired guitar.

"Oh, I just got my girlfriend something for her birthday. Check it out." It was a stuffed animal of a bat. Donny's hair was dyed black and dreadlocked in an awful Rammstein way. He was wearing black UFO pants and had an eyebrow piercing. His girlfriend probably had pale skin and black lipstick and huge boobs and listened to Bauhaus and they probably drank each other's blood on the overpass WE had shared.

I got over my crush on Donny. It took a little crying, a little song- writing, and a few nights of angrily strumming the only song I knew, which was from the Ninth Symphony, and, arguably, the first hardcore.

I never got over my crush on guitars, though. The romance of that electric kiss when you plug into an amp. The hum of the feedback blowing in your ear. The heartbreak of those first notes when the soundcheck ends and the band strikes up brings it all back. Every album is that overpass on the Southern State Parkway. And every track is a different car sailing underneath, oblivious to the moment of teenagers above them bathed in the freedom of night.

# All 4 Love

*Is he sweaty or is he greasy?*
*The moisture is centered on his hairline, so it might be pomade running from his comb-over.*
*Then again, it could also be sweat.*
*Is the act of sitting at an oak desk really enough to burn calories for this man?*
*Am I sweating?*
*Did I forget to put on deodorant this morning?*

The only sure thing was that the red leather chair I was fidgeting in probably cost more than my entire college education. It was soft, high-quality furniture, definitely stitched from newborn animals. I should have felt great sitting there, like a million screaming, suffering bucks, but I felt out of place trying to remember what good posture felt like in an office belonging to someone I was convinced was the most wretched human being on earth.

When I was twenty-one, I spent the summer as cheap labor at a local film studio. I was hired as a receptionist, but I got suckered into a seamstress internship. This meant I worked thirty hours a week for free in addition to my eight hours a day answering phones. My duties also included taking out large industrial trash bags of wet food and sharp objects, killing a colony of silverfish living in a broom closet so I could turn it into a small office, and avoiding the undressing gazes of my three horrible bosses. Each boss was more than a hundred pounds overweight, racist, and incapable of brewing their own coffee. Several times during that summer, I did a butthole finger sweep and stirred their coffee with it in a thoughtful manner, like a mom starting her day off right. They called me "sweet cheeks" and "kid." I scrubbed the urinal with a sponge and washed their mugs with it. They stared at my boobs. I took office supplies in small-scale rebellion, smuggling out teabags and pencils as I felt Nat Turner would have done in another place in time.

I would have quit on the first day if not for the fact that the office was the Studio 54 of C-list local celebrities. I received stern talking-tos when I put Mick Fleetwood on indefinite hold and then again for hiding under my desk when one of the dudes in Zebra sent me out for Starbucks. I just wasn't cut out for life on the outskirts of the long-faded spotlight.

The biggest bright spot in what was otherwise a total blight on my summer was that for three weeks, the studio was in production of a kid's television show. The concept: a lanky, ageless, eerily enthusiastic man in a red, white, and blue leotard wishes himself into the bedroom windows of sleeping fat kids. Then, with the help of his accomplice, a human-sized magical butterfly, the kids teleport to far-off places such as the rainforest or a coral formation under the sea. Along the way, they encounter different species of health-conscious animal friends who teach them about muscle groups and how to stretch. At the end of the show, our hero safely deposits the kids in their beds, where they rub their eyes and wonder if the soreness in their joints was all a dream or a childhood kidnapping fantasy. It was basically the Katie Beers[2] story with a badger playing the roll of the concerned neighbor who tipped off the cops. None of the writers seemed to notice the similarity. I kept my mouth shut, reasoning that I was paid to photocopy scripts, not remind other Long Islanders why Spaceplex[3] isn't there anymore.

At the studio, I was not allowed in the commissary during lunch. Technically, I was supposed to be answering the phone and fisting the inside of the copy machine. I spent the first day of production alone in my office, looking up fetishes on the Internet and smelling the far-off smells of lunch, hesitant to leave my desk. I had already been told earlier in the week not to have my tattoos uncovered in view of the Client. For those who have never worked in an office, the Client is any intangible, easily-offended person or group prone to getting the vapors

---

[2] A Long Island kid, exactly my age, who was kidnapped when I was in the fourth grade, causing my mom to say things like, "If anyone tries to steal you, you have to ask them for a password. If they don't know it, then, well, they're just trying to steal you and you should probably run away."

[3] A psychedelic Chuck E. Cheese. Lucky rich kids had birthday parties there.

when exposed to body art. The Client is bashful, religious, and does not wear jeans. The Client hates flare.

I was told I wasn't allowed to leave my office except to make coffee or unclog the toilet, but at that moment, if someone had dangled a wish and a handful of potato salad in front of me, it would have been a tough call. I stood near the office door, listening for the phones and hoping for a passerby to watch my desk while I ran down the hall to kick the vending machine. After a few minutes, a child ran through the hallway waving a sandwich.

"Hey! Kid!" I shouted.

His pace ground to a halt. "I'm sorry."

It dawned on me that he thought I was *that* sort of adult, the kind that is upset by running or play.

"Oh. No! I'm sorry. I don't care if you're running. I just wanna know your name."

"Ralphie," he said, taking a bite of the American hero. Shreds of lettuce hung from his mouth like mint-waxed dental floss.

"Ralphie, my name's Cassie, and I'll give you five bucks if you can get me a piece of hero just like that."

"Five bucks? Okay!" He tore down the hall, gangly child-star limbs flying out in every direction. I wasn't sure if five dollars was too much or too little to ask. When I was eleven, my parents dared me to eat the chunk of fat from a can of pork and beans for five dollars. I did it, and it had seemed worth it then. Did inflation affect that sort of thing? He seemed happy to help, but he also could have just been fucking with me.

Ralphie returned with a friend, a freckly, blonde boy. "This is Tyler. We got you eggplant, too."

"Whoa! You're the king!" I took a seat at my computer and minimized the Googled photos of tumors on the screen.
"Nice to meet you Tyler. So what do you guys do?"

"We're the actors," Tyler explained.

"How old are you?" I asked.

"I'm ten," Tyler said, bouncing a ball on the ground. "He's eleven."

"I'll be twelve in a month," Ralphie corrected.

"How old are you?" Tyler asked.

I never understood women who were offended by that question. I still counted the months of my age, proud that I hadn't yet died of my own poor choices. "Twenty-one and a half."

"You don't look twenty-one," they said.

"I have a cousin who is seventeen," Ralphie said. "You look about her age."

"I don't smoke. I think that could be part of it. Also I'm probably developmentally delayed."

"How come you have to eat in here all by yourself?" Tyler asked.

I dug into the eggplant like someone opening an airlifted UN ration. "Well, have you met the slimy guy with the nice office? That guy is my boss and he said I can't leave."

"How come?"

"Every time a fat guy needs coffee, I have to fetch it."

"Why can't they just get it themselves?"

"I don't know, but this job is really wearing into my dignity."

"That stinks." I was sure that they understood. They may have been half my age, but we were all underdogs, and we were in this together.

"Tyler, Ralphie. Want to play Uno?"

"YEAH!" After that day, all the child actors began eating lunch in my office. This would not have been a problem, except they were often absent when they were needed for their cues because they were running to my car to get Van Halen CDs and snacks. One day, Ralphie, Tyler, and the rest of the TV gang didn't come to my office at lunch. I saw Tyler in the hall while I was taking a message from somebody's secretary.

"Hey, Tyler!"

Tyler stopped in his tracks and hung back in the hallway. "Hey, Cassie."

"Where'd you guys go?"

"We got in trouble because we missed our cues again. They said they'd dock our pay if we hung out in your office. I like Ratt and Karen Black and all, but my mom is gonna kill me if I don't get paid. You understand, right?"

It felt like a breakup. It wasn't me. It was bad timing. Just try not to cry. "Yeah, Tyler. Of course I understand. We can still IM, right?"

"Yeah, that's totally cool. But we're shooting the jungle scene right now so I gotta go. See ya!" He bounded down the hall and looked back one last time. Soon, all I could see was the brim of his safari hat as he rounded the corner and was gone. These children were like mine canaries for the tenuousness of my job. I knew it was only a matter of time before I was fired.

Across the hall, there were two graphic designers crammed like veal into one tiny office. Gary and Tim had been working for the company for two years. They hated the bosses worse than I did, mostly because they paid thousands of dollars for the skill of graphic design, but were often asked to brew coffee and vacuum in my absence.

"Did you see the fuckbot you cleaned out that closet for?" Gary asked, adding CGI sparkles onto the wings of the human butterfly.

The fuckbot was a new employee I had overheard the bosses talking about. "No," I said, sitting on his desk and eating the ziti he had scored for me. "What's her job?"

"She's gonna do marketing and cold calls to get money to back this bullshit."

"How long do you think she'll last?"

"It's hard to tell. For secretaries, you've lasted the longest out of everybody, and it's only been, what? A month?"

"Two months," I corrected.

"Yeah. There's no way she'll last that long."

The name of the new fuckbot was Carmen. Her complexion had the crisp malignancy of Original Recipe chicken. Her nails were long and talon-like to protect against men in sheer button-down shirts dancing closely at Mulcahy's[4] happy hour. She wore spandex pants, jeweled open-toed heels, and tops that plunged to her belly button. Although my boobs were better than hers, I had outfitted them modestly during my interview with the CEO. I wore a sweater when they told me I would be making ten dollars an hour. Carmen had worn a shiny, J Lo-inspired number, and she started at $35,000 a year. My desk had to be dragged indoors from where it was rusting in the backlot. Hers was Endusted by yours truly.

The sound of Carmen's boots padding down the hall irritated me. They were a telltale heart of where I had gone wrong in life. Somewhere, somehow, my genetic code had split off and

---

4 The Ultimate Long Island Bar and the site of the first show I ever went to. I won tickets on the radio to see Ratt and took my stepdad. Leather-clad women stood on the bar waving their bras. I was a changed person after that night.

made it so that I couldn't be happy with a job serving someone. I wanted nothing more than to be okay with the status quo, with razor-thin cell phones and manicures and boyfriends with dragon tattoos. It wasn't the office I hated. It wasn't the bosses, or Carmen, or heavy garbage bags that ripped and spilled faxes and tuna all over the hall. It was *myself*. I was the star-shaped peg in a world of office partitions and Entenmann's crumb cakes. I was betrayed by my own art-faggy dreams.

"They make porn here, you know," Carmen said. I was elbow-deep in the vending machine, trying to break the plastic flap so I could get a hanging bag of Twizzlers.

"What?"

"They make porn. They have a house in Los Angeles, and they film it there."

"No way!" I said.

"This children's show? Just a front for the porn, to legitimize the company."

"That is *fucking awesome!*"

"I guess. I think it's gross. If I ever caught my fiancé looking at porn, you can bet I'd call off the wedding."

I went to Gary's office and closed the door. "Dude!" I whispered.

Gary looked up from his Mac. "What?"

"Did you know they make porn here?"

"Of course I do. Open this box."

He kicked over a box of DVDs. *All porn.*

"I designed the covers. Thanks, college education."

It wasn't just porn. It was *raunch porn*. The kind with every imaginable fluid being sprayed on someone's face, ass, and pigtails.

"Whoa! This is *awesome!*"

"Trust me. You edit enough shots to the face, they all start to look the same, and it's not so awesome anymore. I can't believe you didn't know about the porn."

Tim walked in and handed me a two-liter bottle of soda he had stolen from the supply of actor food. I chugged it and handed it back to Gary.

"What'd I miss?" Tim asked.

"She didn't know about the porn," Gary said, throwing up his hands in disgust. "How could you not know about the porn?"

I got called into the boss's office before lunchtime. I was stitching bright pink antennas onto a SeaMonkey costume when the CEO called my office line directly. He did not usually move unless prompted by involuntary life functions, meals, or pheromones. For him to pick up a phone and dial my extension meant it was over. I noticed earlier that week that my paid hours had been cut in half, and my freebie "internship time" had doubled. I felt the shadow of the axe about to fall, so I had already accepted a nanny job for the children of the choreographer.

Ian's office had a glossy dark-wood desk, monitors revealing everyone in the building, and an armoire full of porn. A warpath of Atkin's Advantage wrappers littered the floor around the desk, casualties in the battle against carbohydrates. A picture hung on the wall, an eight by ten inscribed, *"2/Ian, All the best–Color Me Badd."* I wondered if the forgivingly multi-racial eyes of Color Me Badd had once looked upon this cheap, greasy display of humanity and sincerely wished him the best.

"Casey," he started off, "I was told that you said I promised you thirty paid hours a week."

"What I said was that thirty hours a week was the minimum I could work. And it's *Cassie*."

"Well, anyway, I never said thirty, so what we're going to do is cut you down to ten."

"That isn't enough money. I have bills to pay." I felt the leather chair getting bigger and absorbing my tiny, insignificant voice.

"Well, I really feel like that's the best option in this situation. Also, we're going to be reevaluating what you do so that you're a little more, and I'm not sure if I'm using the word right here, productive."

*Somewhere in a lab, science is crafting the perfect worker. Males will have tremendous muscles capable of lifting a sewer grate to dive into the murky depths to retrieve a fallen penny. Females will have huge tits with erect, four-inch-long, porn-star nipples. All will have at least six arms for multitasking and will work for praise, heavy petting, or scraps of food.*

"No, you're not using the word correctly, because if I were any more productive, I'd *die*. If that's the best you can do, then consider this my notice." We locked in a moment. I stared at him, then at teen sensations Color Me Badd, then back at him.

"Well, Casey, if that's how you feel, then we wish you all the best."

I cleaned out my desk. Gary and Tim wished me good luck, and we made vague plans to hang out the way well-meaning transient coworkers do. I walked to my car, laying my keys into the side of Ian's BMW.

I started the nanny job a few days later when I dropped the choreographer off at the studio. I got to borrow her SUV for the week while I watched her ten-year-old daughter and teenage son.

"Now, the cat eats a scoop of the dry food once a day and the kittens don't eat anything yet. Monica knows how to feed the birds and the lizard, so she can show you if you get confused. I left money in an envelope on the table for food and the movies."

"Ma, Cassie's not stupid. She's been watching me and Tyler and Ralphie all summer." Monica had been on the show as a backup exerciser. She knew I was a capable nanny as well as a ruthless Uno player.

"Oh, I know! I just get scared. Okay, I gotta go. Love yous! Mwah!" She kissed us both on the cheek and got out of the car. Wilson and Lonnie, the other two obscenely rude heads of the company, appeared behind her.

"We need a ride to the buffet," they said. I looked at the choreographer with eyes that pleaded, *"These fuckers have been sexually harassing me all summer."*

"Cassie, could you just take them to the buffet so I don't have to hear about it?" she asked. I understood the logic: I had a four-minute car ride with them, but she would have an eight-hour plane ride. They opened the door and slid into the backseat. The car listed back-and- forth with the extra weight and I threw it into drive.

"Well, Little Miss Monica," Wilson cooed in a condescending adult voice. "I hear your cat had kittens."

"Yeah!" she said, excited about feline motherhood. "There are six of them!"

"Well, we're going to the *Chineeese* buffet," Wilson said.

"And you know what they eat there?" Lonnie asked.

*"Meow, meow, meow!"* Wilson finished. He and Lonnie laughed hard, wheezing and gripping each other's thighs.

"Monica, don't listen to them. Just hope their hearts give up on the way out of the car." We pulled up to the buffet. "That's enough. Now get out."

Lonnie meowed, and they both started laughing again. "I'm gonna need you to mail this for me today, Cheeks. *Priority*. This is important shit in here," Wilson said. He thrust a package into my hands and they shimmied out of the car.

"Have a nice day, *ladieees*," Lonnie said in an antagonistic Jerry Lewis voice before slamming the door.

There were gleaming blue fountains and wishing pools throughout the shopping center. The biggest one one was surrounded by benches in the middle of the parking lot. I left the SUV running next to it and Monica and I got out.

"Alright, kid. I want you to think of a wish. Like, a really good, expensive, Priority wish for the rest of the year." We stood on the ledge of the fountain and held hands. "Got one?"

"Yep!"

The chlorinated water shone like liquid diamonds, recycling in a vacuum and spraying into the sun.

"Okay. I've got one too. Are you ready?"

"Yep!" She closed her eyes and squeezed my hand.

"One!" I wasn't cut out for office jobs.

"Two!" I hated Xerox machines and paper jams and the smell of toner.

"THREE!" And I would never work for anyone like Ian, Wilson, or Lonnie again.

The little corrugated box floated on the surface of the water. We watched it row itself to the tiled edge of the fountain before it sank to the bottom, the world's smallest failed regatta.

Monica kept holding my hand. "I wished for more kittens when the new kittens get older. What did you wish for?"

"If I told anyone, it wouldn't come true, kid."

## *Tones of Home*

Teenie Beanie Babies took over Long Island in a quick blitzkrieg of collector's delusion. If, when I was in the seventh grade, terrorists had used frogs and weinerdogs filled with plastic beans as part of a calculated biological warfare effort, we'd all be goners and I would not be here, living to tell the tale. My house would have been ground zero, a million little stuffed animals exploding at once in an attack on the freedoms we as Americans enjoy to spend our money on useless things with the assumption that they will accumulate value.

"Whadda you guys want from McDonald's?"

Light filtered through the oak trees into the kitchen window and onto my sister, who was digging in the refrigerator. There was a persistent hope that by closing and reopening the refrigerator door, some kind of molecular repositioning would happen and New Food would appear.

"What don't we have?" Carly yelled to my mother, opening and closing the door again.

"We need Seamore the Seal and Quacks the Duck."

"I thought we *had* Quacks the Duck!"

I was eating Fluff out of the jar, assessing the scene in our kitchen. A shoebox of old lotto tickets sat on the counter next to a spent sleeve of cookies. Paper, empty cans of Pepsi, Barbies in varying states of undress, folded T-shirts that had not yet migrated up the stairs to our rooms, and beanbag animals, still in the plastic. The counters were stacked with crap, and I was at its nexus, drawing a picture of Godzilla destroying my middle school.

I could hear my mother taking a pensive drag on a cigarette. "We *don't* have Quacks the Duck." And then, in a quiet muttered aside, "Jesus *Christ*. It's like they're all *deaf*."

"I'll take Chicken McNuggets, then," Carly said, even though she was already making a peanut butter and jelly sandwich. Carly was bottomless, the type of kid who was always eating but consistently maintained a slim sixty-five pounds. Her metabolism was a vestigial reminder of the few good genes we had floating in the pool, and she proved herself occasionally useful by sucking in her stomach to show her ribs for a sympathy dollar when we could hear the ice cream man on the next block.

My mother cooked once a week, mystery meals whose brown forms were charred into matter indistinguishable from the furniture found around people who died of spontaneous human combustion. We ate McDonald's every other night, pizza on Wednesdays, and KFC if my parents were feeling ambitious enough to drive to the next town. I was a vegetarian, so I either ate hamburger buns with ketchup or Cookie Crisp. Carly had usually already finger-banged every morsel of cereal feeling around in the box for the prize. As a family, we were sluggish, immobile, and quick to turn on each other in fits of carbohydrate rage. We lived simply, communicating only when we needed an extra tub of honey-mustard, and the feeling of completing an entire Happy Meal toy collection was all the validation we needed.

"Are we ever gonna go on vacation?" I said. The loneliness of summer was almost worse than school. I had no friends, and I could feel myself slowly baking to death in my attic room. Every day was secondhand smoke punctuated by episodes of *American Gladiators* and spastic moments alone in the pool, pretending I was the last dolphin on earth.

"You need *money* to go on vacation," my mother said. "Didja get a job or something?"

"Why don't we have a Garage Sale?" Carly suggested.

"You know how Artie feels about *that*." Artie, my stepdad, had once posited the theory that if we had a Garage Sale, strangers would actually break into our garage and make off with his tools, the dad equivalent of a heist at the Louvre. Carly and I had pleaded that wasn't how it worked, that the odds of anyone going rogue in our own driveway and taking things that weren't for sale were slim to none. But my parents tuned us out, returning instead to peeling the plastic off of Slim Jims and watching Nitro chase after Sabre on The Gauntlet.

"Maybe we can ask him again," I said.

"Yeah," Carly chimed in.

"We'll see. Why don't you guys go outside and leave me alone?"

"It's too hot out," we both said, and Carly threw herself dramatically against the refrigerator, fainting.

I didn't have any strong ideas about what I would be like when I grew up. I had vague plans for becoming attractive, but, for the most part, my future was unwritten. My family would not have a computer until the dawning of the next century, so I was untouched by the influences of the Internet or popular culture aside from things I accidentally found. I liked Aerosmith, and my grandpa was always building new things from stuff he got out of people's trash. Other than that, there wasn't anyone else to model myself after. I imagined myself in my twenties riding around on a reassembled lawn mower, multicolored scarves flying in the summer wind, all sexy, half-crazy, and agg-agg-agg-agg-GOW![5]

I was mostly excited about the prospect of the yard sale because it meant an influx of new faces hanging out in our driveway to gawk at our stuff, new character actors in the tired sitcom we acted out day after day as a family. I had never really known anyone to seek out used goods, except for maybe my grandpa, and he was the weirdest person I knew. I felt that I was, at the very least, assured a day of scavengers and social pariahs. Plus, if we made enough money, my parents would take us on a vacation. Usually, we hardly spoke to each other, but vacations brought out our best selves, a real Us-Against-The-World mentality. There were long lines of people to make fun of as we waited for roller coasters, Amish buggies my stepfather tried to race in our Buick, and, just once, we ended up with a room that had a vibrating bed.

"Gimme another quarter!" I had said, taking a coin from my stepdad and putting it into the corroded metal slot where

---

[5] One of the greatest shows I have ever seen was Draw the Line, the Aerosmith tribute band from Boston. All those people, pumping fists, singing the "Let it go" part of the song "What It Takes" was the single most moving moment of my life. God, if you're out there, I'd give it all up, all these riches and fame, just to be in an Aerosmith tribute band for *one day*.

the words "Magic Fingers" were embossed on the outside.

Carly and I flopped backwards onto the mattress, and ole Magic Fingers got to work, shaking the bed frame.

*"Aiaiaiaiaiaiaiai!"* I was nine, and I had no idea what function the bed provided for those more worldly-wise of the magic its trembling fingers could perform, or that perhaps, as an adult, I would think back to this amenity and wish I remembered the name of this motel. In any event, as I laid on the bed next to my vibrating seven-year-old sister, one thing was for certain: what I was experiencing *was magic*.

My mother burst in the door, spoiling our rapture to announce the ice machine was out of order.

"That sucks," my stepdad said, rising from the other non-vibrating bed. "I'm gonna take a crap. Oh, the girls need another quarter."

My mother set to unpacking all of our clothing into the hotel drawers, a move I would later decide in my adult life was a surefire way to get scabies or roaches. But there was something about the way my mother did it that made it official. This was our New Home. I could pretend we now lived in this seedy interstate motel. It was *our* cleaning lady who knocked on the door in the morning and stole change off the dresser. This was how rich people lived, and I was proud.

It wasn't hard to convince my stepdad to have a garage sale after all. Artie took on the challenge of planning a route off Long Island with the same enthusiasm as an innocent man plotting a way of getting out of Alcatraz. He would get home from work, take off his boots, and immediately set to analyzing maps and traffic patterns, watching the weather on the local news the way some study advanced physics: the Belt Parkway, the tunnel, the Goethals, all parts of a puzzle with no solution; a riddle on a cereal box you don't get to solve before your mom throws it away.

The places we went on vacation never made it into the *Baby-Sitter's Club* books I read. In fact, it seemed to me the author, Ann M. Martin, lead a very sheltered life. The babysitters always vacationed together, with monetary concerns and all realities suspended during carefree jaunts to Vail for skiing and the Bahamas for a cruise. It almost seemed like Ann M. Martin was receiving kickbacks from the tourist boards of these cities, and, in doing so, certainly made a lot of actual working-class babysitters have the early realization that not everyone gets to go to Hawaii with their eight best girlfriends.

Carly wasn't a reader, so she had no idea how skewed our future really looked. There was no way of conveying to her that other people, apparently, had separate party clothes and parents who worked in offices and clean houses and ping pong tables and loyal, noble dogs who did not lie under the table panting for gray fish sticks at dinnertime. It was hard for me to gauge how much Carly noticed of how wrong we were, but it did seem like a yard sale was something normal families did, so maybe there was hope.

"Are you gonna sell your Urkel doll?" Carly asked. We were rooting through boxes in the attic, pulling out unwanted old friends and throwing them into bags.

"Yeah, I never even liked him anyway. Are you gonna sell your *Full House* doll?"

"Yeah. Maybe. I dunno." She looked at the nondescript Olsen twin. "Yeah."

We agreed we would not give up any Barbies. I still played with mine, something I did not feel remorseful or lame about, but would never admit to anyone in the cutthroat world of Sagamore Junior High. We poured through boxes of cheap McDonald's toys, Cabbage Patch Kids, and Magic Nursery Babies. Gone, gone, gone.

I was seized with fear when the dreaded box of My Buddy dolls surfaced. At an early age, I had correlated the smirking blinkless glare of My Buddy with Chucky and the soul of demented child-killer Charles Lee Ray. My mother, who stayed at home while we were at school to watch TV and plot new ways to torture us, would sometimes retrieve this doll from the attic and put it in my bed. This was a favorite pastime of hers, shortening our lives one day at a time.

"They have to go," I said, closing my eyes. "But I can't be the one to touch them. They'll *know*."

"You are *such* a doucheburger," Carly said, throwing the brown-haired one in a trash bag.

It was surprising that I hadn't been attacked by My Buddy by now. For my entire life, all of my fears and neurotic child energy had been 100 percent concentrated on my toys. It seemed like scientific fact: that sort of feeling cannot be destroyed, instead it would funnel and pool into the murderous hands of a near life-sized doll. The yard sale could not come soon enough.

Carly tossed her own My Buddy into the bag. "You are *such* a lamewad."

The yard sale itself was full of last-minute revelations. I decided to cast off some precious cassette tapes, like shedding my skin in the hopes of molting into a cooler person. Tapes that did not make the cut included Michael Jackson's *Dangerous,* the self-titled Blind Melon album, and Smashing Pumpkins' *Siamese Dream.* Tapes that I would never part with included Aerosmith's *Toys in the Attic,* Four Non-Blondes' *Bigger, Better, Faster, More!* and Melissa Etheridge's *Yes I Am,* which I listened to on a Walkman from the front seat of the bus every day, fast forwarding and rewinding so that I could hear "Come to My Window" on an endless loop.

My mother was willing to part with a surprising amount of stuff, strapping on a fanny pack full of singles and rolled quarters, wheeling and dealing like a pro. You would have thought she had participated in a lifetime of yard sales from her professionalism and bargaining prowess, but, really, it was her first time.

"That treadmill? Hardly been used. Twenty-five." She unzipped the pouch and fanned a handful of cash. "You know what? For you, today, *twenty.* Can't beat that with a stick."

Cars pulled up in front of the house and slowed down to scope out our junk. Some found it satisfactory and stopped. Others drove away.

"Go on," Carly grumbled, suddenly a hardened businessperson. "We don't want your business anyway."

As a family, we had never so much as slowed down for a yard sale. My mother insisted that you could get bugs from secondhand items, whether these bugs were of a household infestation nature or a close personal crab was unclear. At first, it seemed to me a strange idea that there was a race of people out there who drove around following neon arrows in a quest for other people's unwanted junk. But, as the day wore on, I began to understand. These were people who wore stirrup pants with frosted hair, foreign families where all of the children had rattails, large women in station wagons overflowing with stuff.

It was the most amazing freakshow I had ever seen. From the steps of our house, I watched as they felt at bottoms of oversized pocketbooks for small change. I milled around among them, pretending I was the lady of the house, adjusting the price tag on my old bicycle and moving knickknacks *just so*. There was an energy that flowed between them, these people, a chaotic joy radiating from the core of their being. It excited a caveman impulse to gather, like seeing an unscrambled flash of boob on an old TV and feeling just the slightest bit turned on. The thrill of the hunt was so tangible, you could almost see it, walking around our driveway in high-waisted jean shorts and haggling with my mom.

A beat-up red sedan with a mismatched replacement hood parked across the street. The driver got out and slowly made her way up toward our house. I had just sold four My Buddy dolls to a woman in sweatpants and a Newport visor.

"A dollar. Just take them," I had said, almost frantic that they might choose that moment to knife her and steal my soul. Carly stood off to the side watching the interaction, shaking her head in judgment.

The driver of the red car had a head of Harpo Marx curls in jet black. She was wearing bell-bottoms and a purple tie-dyed Aerosmith shirt. She stopped to look at the table that held our toys. Carly and I were standing next to a Parcheesi set, arguing.

"You shoulda gotten more for those My Buddies."

"I just wanted them gone!" I defended.

"We're trying to go on vacation here, not give everything away. Jeez. Can you try *not to be a herb* for just one second?"

"Scuse me." Female Robert Plant was staring at us.

"What do you want?" Carly snapped, irritated by my lack of business-minded coolness.

"I was just wondering how much this is." I was selling a little purple eagle that balanced on its beak, soaring as if by magic. She took it from its stand and held it so that it was flying on her index finger.

"For you, *right now,* fifty cents," Carly said in her best impression of our mother.

"Sold, man. I'm gonna look at some more stuff. Do you think you can hold my bird for me?"

"Sure!" I said, and took it.

"Thanks, little dude." She walked off toward some old throw

pillows. I heard her say, "Excellent!" and she held up my Blind Melon tape, picking it up and looking at it in a spacey kind of way. She turned back to me. "You got my bird?"

"I got your bird!" I said, winking and pointing, reflecting and refracting the good cheer of the yard sale.

"Awesome!" she said. Carly folded her arms and we both watched her, moving around the small huddles of people, picking up stuff and looking at it as though each item possessed a magic we had never known.

"What a weirdo," Carly said.

"Yeah..." I trailed off, lost in thought. I had never thought about what it meant to be a weirdo, I just knew I felt like everyone in my family had been born weird. To me, we were like X-Men but instead of fast reflexes and useful mutant abilities, we hoarded figurines and electronics. Was it weird to have a house full of unnecessary items, or to drive around in a beat-up car, finding new things to appreciate?

Lady Robert Plant approached Carly and me. She had four mauve-colored throw pillows, a Blind Melon tape, and the human-hair wig my mother bought when she bleached her real hair so blonde she looked albino and didn't want anyone to know.

"This wig is *awesome!*" she said, holding it up.

"Sometimes I put it on and pretend I'm Richard Simmons," I said.

"Our mom hates it. It brings her much shame," Carly said.

"How much for all this? And the bird?"

"How much you got?" Carly said, narrowing her eyes.

"Five bucks?"

"Sold!" I said. "Here's your bird."

"Thanks, dude. You guys have a good day." She gathered the pillows under one arm, put the wig on her head, and walked off toward her car with the bird balanced on her finger. We watched her as she rolled down the windows and started the engine. The belts screeched in the summer heat and she drove away, giving me a wave. The words to "No Rain" hung in the street like exhaust.

"What a weirdo," Carly said, stuffing the money in her fanny pack.

"Yeah," I said. "I guess."

In the end, we made enough money to go on vacation,

Amish country, and got stuck in traffic on the Verrazano Bridge because there is no real way off Long Island. My parents passed the time by chain-smoking with the A/C on high and the windows rolled up, blasting us with a wave of cold, smoky air. Carly and I got into a slap fight over the hump seat in the back of the Buick, and both of us eventually fell asleep with little red handprints on our legs, arms, and faces where each of us had gotten a good one in. I do not know what Carly dreamed about because she didn't read, but I fell asleep thinking about little bars of soap, the things I had that I didn't need, and how weird I might turn out when I grew up.

And when I woke up, we were someplace else, getting along and eating Happy Meals like the families I never read about in books.

# *North Country Blues*

The absence of divine intervention is tricky to detect, like an aneurysm or stroke in someone young and otherwise symptomless. You go through life thinking you are in the bask of a warm God-light that allows you to drive heavy machinery without incident and find loved ones like it was part of a predestined blueprint. God is watching you, winking, smiling like the sun in a Raisin Bran ad, digging two scoops of good fortune and throwing them your way.

But is God really there? Did He plant that wrinkled ten dollar bill in your jacket, or did you just stuff it in your pocket and forget about it? Is He keeping your car on the road when you are feeling under the seat for *Pleased to Meet Me?*

Is that God in the uncomfortable pauses that well up in your ears like saltwater?

Hold the seashell to your ear and hear the loneliness rolling back at you.

"How was work?" The odometer read 180,000 miles. Minus the thirty-eight thousand it came with. Divided by four and a half years, fifty-two weeks in a year. It added up to a small miracle the car was running like a champ after so much devastation, like a billboard of a shark-attack victim turned marathon runner. Determination. Pass it on.

"It was okay." It was always just okay. Never better, seldom worse. The mental meat grind of working a job that was less than the future you had projected for yourself at your current age. Last year, this time, you were working at a bookstore where part of your responsibilities included cleaning the toilets of the public bathroom. There was a calendar that you would pass every day on the way to the restrooms, long-handled brush in hand. The cover was a sad-faced birthday clown that read, "Not everyone gets to be an astronaut." That sentiment stuck in your head as you refilled industrial rolls of toilet paper throughout the Christmas season. You were not an astronaut. You were not even close.

Ahead of you, in traffic, someone throws a wadded-up ball of paper out the window. It is lost to the highway, whipping into oblivion at a speed of seventy-five miles an hour. You wonder what was so urgent to discard out of the window of a moving vehicle at the risk of a thousand dollar fine for littering. That thought is lost into a pool of others–bills, ideas, the division of the next paycheck into needs, wants, and fantasy scenarios that involve rolling in a pile of singles. Somewhere in traffic, the van that threw the paper weaves in and out of cars with a sun-faded sticker declaring God as the manic driver's copilot. In that case, is God white-knuckling the oh-shit-handle, muttering prayers to Himself? Is He unfolding the map, saying, "If you'll slow down a Me-damned minute, maybe I can figure out how to get us where we're going?"

If you had to guess, you would say that God is probably not in North Carolina, that maybe He had a job at the hosiery mill that got outsourced, or sold tires at the old Sears before it closed down. He could just be living off the grid, in a single-wide up on Spencer Mountain, adjusting the bunny ears of an old television set, not knowing about the switch to digital cable. It's better God didn't watch the news anyway. It always made Him cry.

The quiet in your car is filled in by the sound of air flowing through the broken seal of your window. There is also a flapping noise from plastic lifting in the wind whose source you cannot easily identify, and usually forget to inspect once you're out of the car. These noises are like an oval at the bottom of the TV screen with somebody signing in ASL that there should be a conversation here from one human being to another. But no one speaks. Your brain is whirring, and your car talks to you on your quiet ride with another person to get dinner.

"Are you happy?" you ask.

"Sure," they say.

Once the car is parked in front of the restaurant, you look back to make sure you won't be towed or ticketed and see that there is a balled-up sheet of paper stuck in the grill. Before you have even given it a moment's thought, you are already running off to solve the mystery of what the minivan discarded.

"It's porn!" you announce, smoothing out the paper, gawking at a double-sided picture of a barely-legal girl making a frowny face and then lifting up a butt cheek for a peek inside.

The clouds above North Carolina squeeze together and part, revealing a spread-eagle view of a fortunate sun.

"Thanks, God!"

I have done the drive from points west back to New York so many times I can do it with my eyes closed, and if my eyes were closed, I could probably tell by a sixth sense what each billboard was, from signs for JR's Discount Outlet to weird advertisements for vasectomy reversal. On these drives, I can't help but think about when I used to get excited about gas station pickled eggs and long lines of train cars, but that's the price you pay for living a long way from home. When the world is a fast-moving succession of Waffle Houses and Shell stations, you have to entertain yourself.

I fumbled in the back seat for a Sundrop, calling out gang vocals and guitar parts, wailing, shredding, and changing lanes with lightning precision. I do so between long conversations which dip in and out of my head so that occasionally, I self-consciously cover one ear with my hand to signal the presence of a Bluetooth if I feel I am being observed.

"Dumb. That was dumb. I can't believe I did that." I am muttering to myself again and look beside me to the trucker meeting my gaze. I adjust my imaginary communication device, and wordlessly gesture as though I am laughing at a joke being said on the other end of the line.

It has crossed my mind more than once that I might be Actually Crazy, and I have had many out-loud conversations with myself about this possibility.

"Well, it's not like I think there are many of me living in one head," I say and look to my road-trip companion, the Pug, who is curled on the seat of the passenger side. I decide that being responsible for the care of another living being nudges me closer to the "Not Crazy" side, and probably will until the day my name is mentioned on the news between sound bites like, "matted and disheveled" and "layers of remains."

I shrug, whipping past signs for an upcoming rest area, opening a bottle of soda. Since I have been in North Carolina, it has seemed like it stays dark out longer, but maybe North Carolina is just that sort of place, cloudy with permanent twilight. The highways at night are as mysterious as they are monotonous, and my brain jumps track to the houses somewhere past water towers and American flags lit up for nighttime, TVs flickering blue light through mini-blinds, people starting their third-shift days, and people thinking they don't want to get up and do it all over again.

"Why do we do this to ourselves?" I say to the Pug. We pass the next exit sign, and I am squinting, looking out for deer in the shapeless mass of trees. There is a figure standing next to the darkness lit up in my headlights, thumb out. I am driving fast, and they are gone as quickly as I pass them.

"Whoa!" I say to the Pug. "That was *totally* a hitchhiker!" The Pug does not understand high-concept ideas like the possibility of picking up a hitchhiker. I consider it on the way to the next exit, me, the Pug, and the hitchhiker, driving in the Toyota, sharing a laugh. A Kerouac adventure, side by side, trucking it during the second American Depression. I think about the thousand horror movies I have seen where some well-meaning Samaritan picks up the person who makes them their next meal. I weigh it, make a snap decision, and I'm on the overpass, going back in the direction of who-knows-what.

"Well, Pug," I say to the wheezing animal on the seat, "this could go a number of ways. I guess we'll find out which." We pass a Flying J and two Baptist churches on our way back around. We are only about an hour outside of Charlotte, but this is what the culture boils down to out here: dried meats and Jesus Christ.

The Hitchhiker is still waiting near the exit sign. I slow down and stop. She takes an uncomfortable and ghostly long time to walk to my car. I usher the Pug into the back seat, thinking I am less likely to be strangled with piano wire if anything goes down from the passenger side.

"Where are you headed?" I ask. She is somewhere in her early thirties with nice blonde hair, the kind that can do that Pantene Pro V hair-swoop thing without even trying. She is wearing high-waisted jeans, a stained T-shirt, and is carrying an overstuffed duffel bag.

"The beach," she says in a stoned kind of drawl, not making eye contact.

"I can take you as far as I-40 goes. I'm headed to New York. Uh, wait," I say, thinking there should perhaps be some sort of mutual understanding here. "Like, you're not gonna kill me, right?"

"You ain't mean, right?"

"Uh, no. I'm not." There is a pause and we both nod. I pop the trunk and she throws in her bag.

"My name is Cassie," I say, extending my hand as we pull off.

"Lurleen," she says, not especially joyful, more exhausted or exasperated, depending on what her circumstance was.

We drive on in silence. She is scratching at her arms, and I am already starting to psychosomatically itch.

"Uh, so, like, what do you listen to?"

"Whadda you mean?" she says. She is staring straightforward, not breaking her fixed gaze on the road ahead.

"Well, like, what music do you listen to?"

"What do YOU listen to?"

"Uh, rock and roll. Right now we're listening to the radio, but I was listening to Bob Dylan before." She is staring blankly at me, so I explain myself. "He is sort of rock and roll, but a little softer. Uh, folkier? Sometimes rocking, though."

"I listen to *Christian* music," she says. She places a weird emphasis on Christian, as though *Blonde on Blonde* was recorded live from hell.

"Oh. That's cool, too." The road rolls by. It is starting to get foggy. She scratches. I scratch, too.

"So what brings you to the beach?"

"Whadda you mean?"

"Uh, like, well, what's at the beach that you need to get to?"

"Where are YOU going?"

"I'm headed home to New York. I live in Belmont now, but I'm visiting my family."

"I had a friend who went to New York and committed suicide. They found her floating in the water." At this point, I have a pretty clear idea that this isn't going to blossom into anything heartfelt or inspirational. There are different vibe molecules in the air, the kind that resonate like a tuning fork where your decision vibrates down your spine like something you haven't chewed all the way. I picked up a hitchhiker, and now I was going to have to deal with it.

The car fills with silence, and I start to wish for every other kind of uncomfortable silence I have experienced in my life. The Break-Up Silence. The Just Walked In On Your Roommate Watching Porn Silence. The Grandpa Just Shit His Pants at the Thanksgiving Table Silence. All of those silences are walks in the park when compared to The Driving With A Hitchhiker Silence.

Lurleen had a death grip on the passenger-side door handle, and though I try to mention she can put the seat back if she wants, she chooses to sit at a perfect ninety-degree angle, which is disturbing even when a normal person does it. The car is eerily quiet until she starts muttering to herself.

"Uh, did you say something?"

"I...understand...I...just...UNDERSTAND! I UNDERSTAND!"

"Um, understand what?"

"I understand about Good God's love for Good God's People! I understand that Our God is not the God of rock and roll and the sinning and the fornication! I just understand is all!"

*Holy shit. This is just my luck.*

"Uh, okay. Cool. Yeah, I totally understand, too."

"Good God's Good People have been exposed to sinning and rock music and our God is not the God of rock and roll!"

"Uh, huh. I can see how you would say that. Do you want a soda? There's soda in the cooler...."

"You're from New York?" she asks, turning from manic to serious in about half a second.

"Yes."

"Do they have churches in New York?"

This is actually the second time I've been asked if New York has churches, as if after 9/11, it became a smoking hole of rubble and manservant coveting. "Yes, we do."

She considers this for a moment. "I was in Virginia. And I was looking for the hospital, and these little people was coming out of the ground and I just couldn't believe how all these little people could appear like that, and then the motel called the police and told them I was trespassing when I was just standing there looking at all the people. Then the officers, they tried to get me a motel room for the night so I could wash up, cuz I'd been digging behind the hotel where the little people was coming up out of the ground, and I walked away and I opened a door and there were these *old people* hooked up to machines and they looked like *aliens*. Then the next day, I tried finding that room and they was gone. Why would they go and make a room up like that with the old people on the machines if they was just going to take it away in the morning?"

I didn't have an answer. I didn't even have an expression I could make to sum up the dumbstruck terror I was feeling at that moment. Instead, I just nodded and shrugged. No, I did not know why they would make such a room.

"But I know *now*. I understand why Good God's Good People would take my kids and why everybody would tell me I needed help and close their doors and why the man at the rest stop told me I couldn't stay there showing my nakedness in the mirror of the ladies' room. I understand now because *God has a plan*."

"Um, I am gonna pull off because I need to get gas, so, like, if you have to go to the bathroom, you can do it now. I think that's God's plan for this car right now."

There was a Hess station up ahead on the right. I pulled in under the bright lights and saw exactly how aged my hitchhiker was. She had the unlucky kind of face of the trailer people they showed cooking up meth on A&E. Except this was real life, and I was taking her to the beach.

While Lurleen was inside of the gas station mart, I got out my atlas and started examining the route it would take to get her to the beach. Apparently, it would be three hours out of the way. That was three hours of Good God's Good People and maybe being killed. The Pug is cute and all, but he would Judas me in a heartbeat if this lady came out of the gas station with a Hunny Bun. I was fucked.

Lurleen emerged from the gas station, and we both basked in the mothy floodlights of the overhang. "This here map says the beach is kind of way out of the way, so I'm probably just gonna drop you off where I-85 meets Route 40. It should be pretty easy to get a ride to the beach from there."

I got in the car and Lurleen hung outside for a second, staring at my dashboard, wild-eyed with a horrified look on her face. She was muttering again when she got back in the car.

Now, if I were a crappy person, I could have abandoned her

in the middle of nowhere to live out the rest of her life digging for little people behind the Hess. But I felt pretty committed to this mission of taking her to the beach, or as far as I could go before she tried to jerk the wheel or something. So I started up the car, and we hit the highway.

On the second leg of our journey, no one said much, aside from occasional mumbles coming from the passenger side. I pretended I didn't notice, and even turned off the radio so as not to invoke the violent Devil Gods of rock and roll. Despite my efforts, the muttering finally came to a head.

"I'm not. I'm not...not...NOT. NOT! NOT A PORN STAR! I'M NOT!"

"What?!"

"Why you keep stuff like that in your car? That's the temptation of the Devil!"

"What stuff?! What are you talking about?"

"That stuff on your dashboard. That is not for Good God's Good People."

I looked at my dashboard. I hadn't noticed that for the last few weeks I had been driving around with a picture of a naked woman in plain sight, the way others might display a parking pass or Baby On Board that had lost its adhesive. I was so desensitized to women in pigtails and catholic schoolgirl outfits that driving around with pornography stuck to the dash didn't register.

"Oh, shit," I said. "My bad. I'll just throw that in the backseat."

"Why would you drive around with something like that to begin with?"

The truth was, I had no idea. Maybe I was just a pervert. Or maybe my God, the God who gives out free porno to His most loyal lambs, was just different from her God, the one who leaves people to deal with great epiphanies while scratching at their filth-encrusted tatters. It felt like kind of a draw.

"I really have no idea," I said, being honest. Wasn't there a commandment about honesty? Did that win me points?

"I just don't understand...understand...UNDERSTAND. I UNDERSTAND NOW!"

"Hey, alright, look, a gas station! I'm just gonna leave you at this Exxon. It's nice and well-lit, Lurleen, so you will totally be able to find a ride to the beach."

"Uh-huh," she said, side-eyeing me, like the dog you pass at the shelter who knows you don't think he's the one.

I popped the trunk and took out her duffle bag. "I hope everything works out for you."

Lurleen snatched the bag and didn't reply, though I truly meant what I said. She walked off, giving one last angry look to the sinner who brought her to the junction of I-85 and Route 40, and I drove off. The Pug resumed his spot in the front seat and fell asleep. I scratched at the case of placebo scabies I was sure I had gotten, keeping my eyes on the road, wondering whose prayers it was God was answering if not the ones most lost in this universe, moths fluttering toward something so bright they can't see what it is.

# *Lucky Town*

*There is a magnetic quality to any roadside attraction where the sign telling you of its existence looks as though it has been etched by the wind. The sign for Calico Ghost Town is particularly time-bitten and attractive, a desert rose on the California Coast, the perfect distraction for the tired brain that has been piloting a moving vehicle for over eighteen sleepless hours.*

My car climbed slowly up a desert mountain, past Airstream trailers shining like foil in the sun, past a limping stray dog that tried to bite me when I stopped to lure it into my car, past giant cacti leaning on themselves in the heat. And when I finally got to the top of the oxidated, sienna canyon, I knew I had hit my El Dorado: Calico Ghost Town is the mothership of tourist traps.

Just under old-timey signs on the List of Stuff I Have to Stop and Look At are cheap, manufactured souvenirs. Although I have little tolerance for snow globes of the Statue of Liberty waving the welcoming green arms of a better life, I can sit for hours in a gift shop in the middle of nowhere fingering the stitches of a leather change purse and admiring the understatement of the "NM" stamped on it in gold letters. I get this from my mother, who is capable of hanging onto the same keychain for twenty years, coveting it as though it were a first-degree relic.

I paid my admission to the ghost town and climbed a hill from the parking lot. I milled around from gift shop to gift shop, comparing geodes, panning for fool's gold, and gawking at the balding tourists and their expressionless trophy wives. There seemed to be something magnetic about what had brought me there, but I couldn't put my finger on what.

Until I saw the animatronic fortune-telling '49-er.

In spite of the fact that I have seen the episode of *The Twilight Zone* with William Shatner and the bobblehead devil fortune-teller a hundred times, no amount of rational thought will sway me into thinking that little paper fortunes are not loaded with celestial merit. This also comes from my mother, who would choose a potentially winning scratch-off over a dialysis treatment for one of her children if it came down to it. It is best that I have not forayed into the world of gambling, as I definitely have a misguided predilection for hoping I am lucky. But, left to my own devices in the middle of the desert, I dug in my bag for my two luckiest quarters.

"YEEE-HAWWW!" hooted a voice box somewhere within the glass chamber holding the PVC soothsayer. The mannequin's eyes rolled back and his head swiveled from side to side, jaws flapping as though he were in the throes of a stroke. *"It's time to live life to the fullest!"* His hands gestured wildly, shaking around a pickaxe, and it seemed more like he was offering a clever one-liner before he broke through the glass and plunged it into my skull. *"YEEEE! You owe it to yerself to get into the gift shop and buy yerself somethin' reeeeal nicelike!"* He froze suddenly, and his long, gray synthetic hair swayed like wheat.

A yellow ticket laboriously printed at the bottom of the machine. I tore it off and eagerly gazed upon my fate:

*Unexpected wealth will arrive.*
*Remember he is richest, who is content with least.*
*When riches come, do not forget that man's true wealth*
*is the good he does in the world.*
*So, when opportunity knocks, grab it.*
*It is easy at any moment to resign*
*the possession of great fortune;*
*to acquire it is difficult and arduous.*

On my trip, I did not find so much as a nickel in the street. In fact, I am pretty sure I lost fifty dollars in cash while digging in my pocket to buy a sticky hand at a Ralph's Grocery. But, I remained optimistic. I'm sure most gold-panning '49-ers did not achieve their wealth instantly. It probably took, like, days to find a brick of gold. Maybe even weeks. And as the fortune said, to acquire wealth was difficult and arduous. I just had to keep at it, whatever "it" was.

★

I was on my way to Manhattan for a job interview, talking sweetly to the little yellow fortune.

"Look. I've been home for two weeks. I'm running out of money and I need a fucking job. It's time to put your money where your mouth is and quit jerking me around."

Since I got home from California, I had been scouring Craigslist for employment opportunities. I was only going to be home for another three weeks before moving to Austin, and finding acceptable temporary employment was proving to be difficult. One lonely night, I answered two ads for writers. One was for a website that needed people to review gay porn. I sent them some writing samples and said that although as a straight woman, I may seem like an unlikely candidate for such a position, in fact I had been judging penises through the harsh lens of reality since I became sexually active, so I was really an ideal candidate.

I did not hear back from them.

I did, however, hear back from a magazine that was looking for people to review adult novelties. Although it wasn't a paid writing position, it was better than the writing position I already had, which involved wearing duck pajamas and chuckling at my own jokes in my parents' living room with no preconceived notions of sexiness whatsoever. Plus, I didn't have to go to the local porn shop anymore and deal with old men trying to commit my boobs to memory while I struggled to compare prices on Doc Johnson vibrators in peace. I sent a few witty replies to the editor, and I was in. I had to be in midtown by six, but I went into the city early to try to arrange a farewell reading at the radical bookstore.

I usually scope out the zines at bookstores out of a sense of duty. I feel that because I went through the effort to make a chapbook, I should patronize other people's creations. Usually, though, the works I end up picking are pretentious exercises in abuse of the Xerox facilities at NYU. A middle-aged man was flipping through the zines, so I figured I would point him in the right direction.

"That one's pretty great. And I'm mostly saying that because it's mine."

"I will check it out," he said, picking it up. He had a middle-eastern accent and was holding several history books. "Can I recommend something to you as well?"

"Yeah, man. I've got time to kill."

He took a book from the armload he was carrying. "This one is the most objective account of Palestinian and Israeli history one can find."

I only had two hours before my interview and that sounded like a tall order. "Uh, mine's about rock stories. Uh, American rock and roll."

He nodded, and we went back to our adjacent tables and coffee. It was clear that neither of us had any interest in the other's recommendations, but for the next half hour, we pretended to read in a strange game of chicken. He periodically closed the book as though he were drinking it all in. I, however, had a feeling that he had no idea who Weird Al[6] was or why I would be describing his sex life in the form of a poem. But, for some reason, I feared this stranger's judgment.

"Mmmm," I said thoughtfully, occasionally mouthing the word 'genocide' with a pensive look on my face.[7]

Once I set up the reading, I stepped out into the street and walked to my car. As it was being ticketed.

"It's cool!" I said. "I'm here. You don't have to ticket it. I'll just take it right out of your way." I felt like a parent trying to get a statutory rape charge dropped against their son.

"You drive away, they just gonna mail it to you," said the sassy, indignant meter maid.

"That's great. I'll just wait here then. Thank you." For an uncomfortable moment, I stood there, impotent to the power of the New York City Parking Violations Bureau. She handed me the ticket.

"Thank you. I appreciate this very much. You will be rewarded for this one day," I predicted as my clairvoyant jaws clapped shut and the cold, February wind rustled the malevolent orange envelope.

---

6 When I worked at the record store, it blew my mind every time someone came in to buy a Weird Al record in the 2000's. How many times can you listen to "My Bologna" without having a moment of self-reflection where you decide that life isn't worth living, nothing is funny, and everything you believe in is a lie? My guess is twice.

7 When I am talking to intellectual people, I usually get by on my knowledge of plot synopses of old *Wishbone* episodes. If the conversation goes beyond that, beads of perspiration form along my hairline and I cheerfully excuse myself.

Once in my car, I reflected on my shrinking bank account balance, and made the decision that New York City parking tickets no longer applied to me. In my head, I was already a citizen of Austin. Until I moved, I was going to live on the fringes of what the Parking Violations Bureau considered acceptable places to leave my car. "Take your little orange threat and shove it, New York!"

This decision should have been enough to keep me from stewing in anger, but I continued to talk to myself and reconstruct the conversation with the meter maid until I had run her over several times in my mind. One would think it would take more than a sixty-five dollar ticket to motivate me plot somebody's death, but that just isn't so. Life did not fall into perspective until I saw a kid with leukemia waiting in a wheelchair outside of a hospital on my drive. Then I remembered what the yellow paper fortune said, and I felt like an asshole. We're all little ants, running around, doing our jobs. Some of us write little ant stories, some of us ticket little ant cars, but nothing is worth having a total meltdown over.

I had calmed down by the time I found the office of the sex magazine. I was extra cautious to park in a zone that would render me invisible to the scrutiny of The Man. I got a receipt from the Munimeter, displayed it boldly on the dash, and ran off to my interview.

The instructions I was given by the editor seemed a bit shady, as she had told me not to mention the magazine's name in the building. The odds were in favor of me being forced to become a drug mule or an escort, and I could have been persuaded to do either if I were being paid. The building seemed fancy, with two doormen, a glass entrance, and a gilded lobby.

When I asked for the fourth floor offices, the doorman did not look at me suspiciously or try to warn me away. After a quick elevator ride, I saw there were leather couches in the waiting area, which to me said that everything was on the up-and-up. I heard someone calling my name from the other side of the lobby. The editor for the magazine was maybe a year or two older than I was, but something about our life paths had diverged so that she was well-paid, and I was willing to insert objects inside of myself to see my name in print. We sat down at a glossy cherrywood table.

"So why do you want to do this?" she asked.

*Desperation? Poor educational decisions? I've reached a roadblock in my potential?* There were too many right answers. "Well, I'm a humor writer, and this seems like a great opportunity. Some would say that I am the Erma Bombeck of weiners and 'giners, so this is probably an ideal match." *Did I really just say that? What have I become?*

"So, you're a fiction writer?"

"Uh, did you read what I sent you? It's all true, friend. Every unsavory detail."

"What do they call that? Creative nonfiction?"

"Something like that. I would call it the painful, sexually-explicit truth." Although I was physically present, my brain was hovering over my body like a baby angel, watching myself participate in this interview. *Wow. What an asshole. An honest-to-god, cross-my-heart asshole. Way to blow it.*

"So, this job requires the use of various sex toys. You rate them on a scale of one to five. Nothing gets a zero, because the company is getting paid to do the review. You can give things a half point, but generally, we try to avoid a score of less than one."

"One means I got a rash from it, right?" I was really on a roll.

"Well, even if the reviewer gets a rash, they're expected to emphasize that not everyone may get a rash from the product. And you have to review every product you pick up. Otherwise we have to call and harass you to get it back, which nobody wants. What sort of adult novelties have you used in the past?"

"Vibrators, mainly. Well, exclusively. Nothing double-sided or anything."

"Well, are you open to using other products?"

"Sure. You only live once, right?"

"Right." There was a pause. "Well, you've got the job if you want it. I just need to make a copy of your I.D. and you can be on your way."

"Great. Let's go for it." I handed her my license.

She stared at it. "Is that a wig?"

"Nope. Just bad genes."

"I see." She disappeared into a back room. During the interview, two men had wandered in. One went into the back room. The other took a seat at the board table with a laptop. He looked like the singer of Midnight Oil if he were partially decomposed.

"What are you here for?" I asked, incapable of minding my own business.

"I'm a programmer," he answered in a voice that suggested he was being controlled from beyond the grave. "Are you a designer?"

"I'm a writer."

"Oh." His tone implied he knew exactly what I was writing, and our conversation ended there.

The editor came back. "Can you come back on Saturday to fill out some paperwork?"

"Sure can."

"You look like a stand-up comedian," she said, giving me a hard stare. I had made the executive decision that any job that may require me to put something in my butt to test it out did not require dress clothes for the interview. I was wearing a western shirt, jeans, and sneakers. Basically, she was saying I looked like Bob Saget.

"I'm not sure how to take that, but thank you. See you Saturday."

I made my way to the elevator and down to the street. I had just scored a real, unpaid writing job. It was like using a box cutter to break the screen on the window of opportunity. Soon, I might actually have a means of paying my student loans. I might even reach a point where a parking ticket would not mean total bankruptcy!

High on life, I called my best friend Colin to tell him the news. "Dude, I'm gonna need you to pick up some stuff for me after I move."

"Fuck you, Sneider! I hope it's anal beads every time!" Colin was unhappy with the idea of me moving.

"I'll PayPal you if you ship them to me," I offered.

"And I hope they're made out of steel wool and barbed wire. Eat a bag of dicks!" My biggest cheerleader hung up on me. I walked to my car, still delighted and ready to take on the world. It was probably the coldest day of the year, so I was eager to get back to my vehicle to dodge the intense wind chill.

When I rounded the corner, I looked down the block, bewildered, and then up the other way.

"Where the fuck is my car?"

I closed my eyes and opened them again, hoping it would be like the Christmas morning scene in every Shirley Temple movie where my car would be gleaming in Technicolor brilliance next to a plate of teacakes, my long-lost fighter-pilot dad, and new puppy.

No car.

Although I had parked in an area I was certain was safe from the parking authority, my car was gone. In its place was an empty coffee cup. I expected to find a note from the Joker rolled up inside it, and I would have to use my powers of deductive reasoning to crack the riddle and find the undisclosed location where my car was being kept.

There was a hot dog vendor on the corner where I stood looking up and down 38th Street as if I was following the puck at a hockey game. "Excuse me. Did you happen to notice a red car, like, right there about ten minutes ago?"

The vendor was so old he looked wise, and it seemed as though whatever he was about to say had the potential to alter the course of my life forever. "Took it," he said slowly, shaking his head like he had just witnessed a suicide bombing.

"Took it where?" I asked, helpless.

"River," he answered, bowing his head.

"How do I get there?" I asked, manic and not quite sure at what point I should start to cry.

"River," he said again, gesturing west on 38th Street. I wanted him to throw an acorn upward that would turn into a dove and fly in the direction that I needed to go.

"River. Thank you, sir." I left my friend and headed toward the river.

My car was towed on 6th Avenue. According to the automated lady on the phone, the impound lot was on 12th Avenue. Also, according to the real human I eventually got on the phone, my car was not received into the lot and they had no record of it being towed. Potentially, it was up on blocks in a chop shop and some hood was taking out my stereo and manhandling the little stuffed hot dogs that dangled from my rearview.

Although I was slowly freezing to death as I walked to the river, I was in high spirits. This was the most exciting day of my life. Not only was I now almost a real adult with an almost real adult job that involved real adult novelties, I was about to inherit a boatload of real adult problems! I was pretty sure that the court hearing I missed a few months back from running a red light was about to be dredged up. Then I remembered that in every Bruce Springsteen song, the River is where the dude's girlfriend gets knocked up, he has to get a job working construction, and the whole fucking economy falls into a recession.

Maybe today I would bring America to its knees. Sweet!

I made it to 11th Avenue with my teeth chattering to find 38th Street was closed off. There was a police car on the corner. I walked toward it and the officer rolled down the window.

"Um, excuse me. What do I do if my car has been unjustly taken?"

"Unjustly taken?" asked the officer.

"Like, stolen or towed. Who knows which, cuz the lady from the impound lot had no idea!"

"Wow. You're freezing."

"No kidding. I'm surprised my spit hasn't frozen my mouth closed," I said, unable to mask my true self.

"Get in the car. We'll make a few calls," they said.

Once I was warm, I was able to appreciate the situation I found myself in. Both police officers were my age, and both looked like Chippendales.

*I'm the luckiest girl in the whole world!* I thought in a Hayley Mills voice.

"Where you from?" asked the one in the passenger seat.

"Long Island," I said, hoping I wasn't visibly snotting.

"No kidding! So are we! Where?"

"Ronkonkoma," I replied, trying to get a glimpse of my reflection in the sheen of the silver cage.

"I'm from Mastic!" said the passenger-side officer.

"We're neighbors!" I cheered.

"Hey, what year'd you graduate? Sachem High, right?"

"2001. Why? Who do you know?" Although there are virtually no benefits to being a Long Islander aside from a slammin' accent, in the company of other Long Islanders, there is always the *Where Did You Go To School and Who Do You Know? Game*.

"My brother's fiancée went there. Hey, we located your car!"

"Aw, man. Thanks, guys. You really saved me from freezing to death. How do I get to the impound lot?"

"Ah, don't mention it," said the one in the passenger seat. "We'll drive you there!"

"Oh, you don't have to go out of your way."

"Hey," said the driver. "Be glad you got picked up by the two coolest cops in New York City." Something about their boyish, helpful jubilance reminded me of Corey Feldman in *The 'Burbs*, a movie that I definitely jerked it to in my formative years. It was gonna be a long night once I got home.

They dropped me off at the impound lot, and once up the stairs, I was repelled by the total vortex of negative energy. It was dead silent, save the shuffling of paper behind the glass and the occasional "motherfuckers" whispered into a Nextel from the peanut gallery. Poor people, the well-off, young and old lined up in the orange bucket seats, in Ecko bubble jackets and rabbit fur coats alike, all thinking one thing: *This is going to cost at least $185.00.*

I gave the lady at the window my information, and she said my car hadn't come in yet. I took a seat next to a man that looked to be about sixty.

"What time did you get towed?" I asked, hoping my team attitude might be the morale boost the room needed.

"Four."

It was now seven-thirty. I rustled around in my bag for a book and remembered the first thought I had had upon waking up: *"I really wish I had a quiet place to read today!"* I said, standing up in an Iron Maiden *Powerslave* shirt to stretch and wipe the sleep from my eyes.

I snickered, loud enough for the woman with a babushka to turn around and shoot me a curious, but still miserable look. It was a lot like the waiting room in *Beetlejuice*.

"What time did your car get towed?" said the guy next to me. He was well-dressed and professional looking, but he was a natural redhead, which counted against him.

"Six, six-thirty. Somewhere in there. How about you?"

"Four. But I figured I'd get some free parking out of it if I was paying for it anyway, so I went to a couple of meetings and showed up about ten minutes ago. It's still not here, though."

"Man. They sure don't get the lead out when it comes to other people's shit," I said.

"That's for fucking sure," he replied. I read for a while, but I was having a hard time concentrating on my book when the human factor of what was happening around me was so awesome.

Two teen girls were talking to a middle-aged fat guy about their recent excursion breaking into the abandoned mental institution at Kings Park. He feigned interest, bobbing his head up and down every so often while staring at their underdeveloped breasts. A balding dad was telling a sob story about how his father-in-law owned his son's car, but he was in the hospital so could they please just reclaim the car? The son stood beside him with a matching sloping forehead. Both were wearing gray sweatpants and Yankees shirts. They were like New York souvenir bookends.

"There are a lot of one-act plays happening in this room," said the redhead beside me.

"You're not kidding, pal."

"CASSIE J. SNEIDER!" said a voice behind the glass.

"Good luck, buddy. Fight the power!" I said, snatching my bag and running to the window.

I gladly paid the hundred and eighty-five dollars. By that point, everything felt like a blessing. Every breath, every movement, every credit card transaction. It felt like my eyes were opened to what life really is: a chain of stupid events that don't matter anyway. By the time I was sitting on the duct-taped seat of the New York City Traffic Violations Bureau shuttle, shouting, "That's it! The red Toyota! The one with the chips in the windshield and the broken bumper and the missing hubcap!" I finally understood that the luckiest person is content with the least.

# A Woman Soon

The first time I got my period, I was sure I was dying, but it wasn't for lack of knowledge on the topic of menstruation. I had already learned about it in school on the day when all the boys were sent to the gym to play basketball. Once the girls were segregated, the school nurse rolled a television into our fifth-grade classroom. Then, for thirty minutes, we were manipulated by a video about a girl who wanted to get her period so she could be "normal." The actress was also in the popular television show *Salute Your Shorts*, and her bouncy curls and overalls immediately won the attention of the class.

In the movie, she asked several trusted adults for help, as though one of them might be willing to inject her with bovine growth hormone or prod her genitals with a sharp stick to speed up the process. In the dramatic conclusion, she bleeds onto her shorts and, thanks to the magic of Hollywood, she begins to blossom from an ungainly child I could actually identify with into a glowing young woman with thick blue eye shadow.

When the school nurse handed me my free Period Pack, I shoved it to the back of my desk, afraid that if I looked at it, I would start gushing blood onto my sweatpants. When my mother picked me up from school and asked how my day was, I didn't answer.

*"I just want to be eleven, for fuck's sake!"* I wanted to scream.

When I got home, I threw the Period Pack under my bed. I hoped it would mutate into some kind of sterilizing cancerous mushroom that would stunt my growth and keep me from developing.

"Is that your granddaughter?" adults would ask my parents in the year 2035.

"No. It's our fifty-three-year-old daughter. She has some

kind of gland thing."

A few months later, my eight-year-old neighbor, Mallory, roller-bladed down the block to where I was playing in my driveway. I was immersed in an elaborate game in which I was a world-renown birdwatcher, lying in the grass alone with my binoculars. Mallory was the kid down the block my sister played with. Her furniture was girly, she had a parakeet named Jonathan Brandis, and she and my sister set her front yard on fire playing with matches.

"How old are you?" she asked, huffing and puffing on her gay pink rollerblades.

"Go away, Mallory!" Her wheezing was making the birds fly out of view.

"Howoldareyou? Howoldareyou? Howoldareyou?"

"I'm eleven. Now go away!"

"My mom says you're gonna get your period soon." Mallory rollerbladed home, where the burned spot on the lawn had just begun to grow back. I dropped my binoculars and ran up the driveway to my house. Once inside, I hid in my closet for several hours, praying quietly that God would never let it happen. My knowledge of God's awesome power was just as good as my knowledge of the human body. My mother had sent my sister Carly and me to Vacation Bible Camp the summer before, not out of any religious zeal, but for a few quiet hours of *The Sally Jesse Raphael Show* and a pedicure by the pool. Carly and I were easily duped into this. We had learned from TV that camp was full of food fights and capture the flag, so we had no cause for alarm.

On the first day, we were ushered into pews and the minister began his sermon with the story of the slaughter of the firstborn children of Egypt.

"I'm firstborn!" I whispered to Carly in a panic, experiencing my first anxiety attack at that very moment. The minister continued and broke off into song.

"Good news! Good news! Christ died for me!" he chanted, and, to our surprise, every child in the church sang along to the morbid chorus. "I'm saved eternally! That's wonderful, extra good news!"

Our summer afternoons, previously full of Super Soakers and water balloon fights, turned into a Sid and Marty Krofft production of Dante's *Inferno*. Arts and crafts time found us coloring pictures of happy lambs that had no idea they were about to be bludgeoned in a sacrifice to a bipolar, spiteful God. We were each given an extra red crayon for the lambs and Carly choked back tears. I finished coloring Jesus and tried to determine what time it was, but I did not have a watch and the sun did not shine in the musty church basement. We sat in uncomfortable silence and listened to the chatter of the eternally saved surrounding us.

Not soon enough, the day was over, the sun had set, and we went home with the best portion of the day wasted. That night I decided to pray for the first time ever.

"Dear God. I do not have any sheep. Please don't kill me. Amen. Also, please don't make me go back there ever again, and I won't do anything bad for the rest of my life. Double amen. Whoa Jesus." I decided that I probably would get better results if I prayed every night instead of just when I needed something, that way God would know I meant business, and I wasn't just being selfish. Also, I figured throwing in a "Whoa Jesus" would ensure me a spot in the Kingdom of Heaven. This system worked well, and I occasionally threw in well-wishes for deceased hamsters or trips to Disney World.

"Dear God," I began, crouched in my closet with my face buried in scratchy turtlenecks and Tasmanian Devil sweatshirts. "Please make it so I can't have babies. I don't want them. Ever. And I don't want to bleed on my shorts. I only have two pairs, and my mom says Didi Seven[8] is too expensive. Amen."

Despite my prayers, each time I took off my pants after that day, I expected a scene out of *The Shining*. Womanhood was some sort of awful punishment, and I awaited the onset of puberty like Marie Antoinette wincing in anticipation of the guillotine. I was determined to stay a child for as long as my dormant reproductive organs would allow. That wasn't too hard, considering my sister and I were mainly outfitted in well-meaning gifts by relatives who seemed to be both blind and foreign.

I also watched a lot of reruns, and when it was time for me to move onto junior high, I was painfully out of touch with what

---

8 A chemical stain-removing agent advertised during *Mr. Wizard* reruns at 6:00 a.m. whose target market seemed to be serial killers due to its blood-removal properties.

human beings my age actually wore.

"Mommy," I said, standing amid aisles of stretch pants in the Pretty Plus section of the Sears children's department, "I think I want to wear jeans this year."

Delighted that I was making strides toward normalcy, my mother ushered me into the juniors department, and there, I made the first decision of my teenage life.

And that decision was to let my mom pick out jeans for me. Skin-tight, straight-leg, store-brand jeans. Jeans with an eighteen-inch zipper that covered my belly-button and cut off the circulation to my genitals if I made the mistake of bending. Jeans that looked like I was trying to score hash at a Rolling Stones concert, not join the science club or contribute to the literary magazine.

"Dear God," I said later that night, hugging my stuffed rabbit. "Thank you for these jeans. I am very nervous about junior high, but I know I will make friends now!" Moonlight shone across my closet and made the copper rivets of my new jeans flash like diamonds. I would finally have friends in junior high. The world would be my denim oyster.

During the summer of 1995, every child entering junior high received a memo in the mail. Mine was confused for a voter registration form and torn in half by my parents, but in subsequent years, I have been able to piece together what it said:

*Dear Prospective Student,*

*You are about to enter a hellish, grueling world where the content of your character is no longer up for consideration. Your social standing from this day forward will be based solely upon the bagginess of your jeans on the first day of middle school. We ask that you shop wisely in an effort to prevent being chewed up and spit out by your peers.*

*Sincerely yours,*
*William Q. O'Brien,*
*Superintendent of Schools*

(For most people, junior high is a miserable experience. If it wasn't, you were probably the asshole who threw pencils out the bus window and spoke at an ostentatious volume about your experience fingering a girl. If so, you also have no business reading about my shitty childhood and should instead do us all a favor and drink yourself to death at a Sublime tribute concert. For the rest of you, please read on.)

Several factors came together during middle school to make them the worst years of my life. First, in seventh grade, I was sent to a different school than my best friend Kristy. Secondly, during the year we were apart, Kristy began to acquire pricey designer clothing, whereas I continued to dress like a German tourist. Lastly, somebody stole my glasses in the seventh grade. I don't know what purpose they could serve to anyone other than me, perhaps as an ant-burning device or inspiration for a custodial circle-jerk, but I never got them back. Instead of buying me a new pair so I could see the chalkboard or watch Nickelodeon without getting a tension headache, my parents refused to buy me new glasses for a whole year. Most of the seventh grade was spent stumbling to the lost and found, feeling the walls of the bright yellow hallway and dodging shapes of people.

I changed schools in the eighth grade, and on the first day, Kristy convinced me to join a club.

"I was in this club last year and we went on all these nature hikes and stuff," she said, rustling around in her new Perry Ellis bubble coat.

"What's it called?" I asked, stuffing my embarrassing Jets Starter jacket into my locker.

"The Outing Club," she said. I was unaware of the potentially far-reaching negative social consequences of joining an organization called The Outing Club. I liked animals. I liked being outdoors. It only seemed like serendipity that I should join such a club.[9]

We had our first meeting after the club fair. The ratio of smelly kids in The Outing Club was probably higher than that of the 4-H Club. In fact, most of the other members appeared as though their parents routinely neglected them. At the first meeting, duties were assigned to each member for the year. I chose the job of feeding the birds in the courtyard an hour before school started. That way, I could satiate my burning need for wildlife and also make an unnecessary spectacle of myself as my peers filed into school. Kristy did not sign up for any

---

9 I distinctly remember my mother making a "who farted?" look when I told her I joined the Outing Club. Then she asked if I was outing myself, and I had no idea what she was talking about.

responsibilities and said that there were a lot more cool people the previous year. There was a tone in her voice that suggested maybe she did not belong among the flannel-wearing underdogs of The New Outing Club.

When my parents finally took me to get glasses, I spent the car ride to the optometrist thinking about all the things that had changed between Kristy and me. She had forgotten my birthday, wouldn't sit next to me on the bus anymore, and refused to be seen without her bright yellow Perry Ellis puffy coat. If only I could do something to make her see I was cool too! If only there was some object I could acquire to tell the whole world I was awesome!

When we got to the eye doctor, a heavenly spotlight fell on the first display I saw: Perry Ellis frames. That was it. It didn't matter that they were men's glasses, that they were too big for my face, or that no one would ever see where it was imprinted PERRY ELLIS MENS on the inside by the ear. I felt that anyone truly cool would be able automatically to sense that the frames bore a designer's name. Then they would invite me to the back of the bus and "have my back," something I had heard cool kids say but never understood its meaning.

No one told me that the frames were not cool, that they obscured my gender, or that they, coupled with the cassette of Melissa Ethridge's *Yes I Am* I listened to on the bus every morning would not ever make my life any easier. But that day, I went home ecstatic.

"Dear God. Thank you for my new glasses. I know it will happen this time. I'm gonna make friends. This is the first day of the rest of my life. Thank you, God. Amen."

I stopped wearing my new glasses about as quickly as I received them. When I saw my reflection in the swiveling mirror at the eye doctor a week later, I knew the magnitude of the mistake I had made.[10] I wore them in school only after the teacher turned off the lights to copy notes from a projector. I wore them at home to watch television. I squinted whenever I could, guessing at the letters and shapes I was bombarded with, using sounds and vibrations to get by, like a bat, or, perhaps, Stevie Wonder.

I was fourteen when I finally got my period. I was gearing

---

10 To date, this remains the dumbest decision I have ever made.

up for a science class field trip to an organic farm and waiting for my mom to take me to buy for the bus ride. I felt a change in the climate of the high-waisted bloomers my mom bought for me, and it had happened.

"I'm dying. There is no God, and I am dying," I said, staring at the crime scene before me.

I tried on a pad, but the only other menstruating adult in the house was my mother. The thing about moms is that they are content with any sanitary napkin, even if it has the dimensions of the Yellow Pages, as long as it is on sale. "This is not acceptable. This cannot be normal. There has to be something else out there." I was talking to myself in the bathroom, trying to decide if it was normal to feel like I was smuggling *War and Peace* between my thighs, when my mom started banging on the door.

"Are you ready?"

"Just a minute," I said, shifting the diaper and trying to walk.

"I don't have all day!"

I decided that it was as comfortable as it was going to get and met my mother outside. Once in the drugstore, I found *Mad Magazine,* but I felt like I was supposed to tell my mother what had happened. In the video I had seen in school, the girl's mother told her she was a woman and hugged her. I was mortified, but I felt contractually obligated to fill my mom in.

I squinted down the aisles of the drugstore, trying to find a shape that looked like my mom. I eventually identified her by straining my eyes, as well as by scent and vibration.

"You done?" she asked.

"Ma, I, uh…." I was too embarrassed to say it. Not only had God abandoned me in my prayers for infertility, but I was now supposed to announce it. I looked around, squinting at the objects for sale when I determined the aisle we were standing in front of contained brightly-colored rectangles. We were right next to the maxi-pad aisle! I need only to gesture for my mother to understand I was now a woman. "Ma, uh, I…" I pointed, lowering my eyes in shame.

"You what?" She followed my pantomime to the colorful plastic rectangles. "You pissed yourself?"

"What?" I squinted harder and read the words on a green rectangle: DEPENDS. "No! I, uh, I mean I…" I moved to the next aisle, a corridor of pink squares.

"You got your period?"

"Uh, I, yeah."

*"I'm very proud of you,"* says Educational Video Mom. *"You're a woman now."*

"We have pads at home," said my mom. "Let's pay for your magazine and get out of here."

I never quite adapted to the height and bulk of my mother's store-brand sanitary napkins. I also never understood why God would ignore such a simple prayer when I was so gracious about my own sterilization. But, wisdom is blind, and perhaps one day when my life is saved by using a Kotex Overnight as a floatation device and by eating my own clotted blood as I await rescue, I will finally understand.

## *Used Cars*

Often youngsters will ask me for advice.

"Cassie J. Sneider," they say, wide-eyed and star-struck. "How can I be more like you?"

The answer is simple: extend your college career for as long as possible by working all day and rock and rolling all night. My college years were marked by denial alternated by deep pride in the ability to function on a half an hour of sleep wedged somewhere between going to class, working full time, and a karaoke habit that my boyfriend, Dave, began to refer to as an "illness," no less problematic than Crohn's or schizophrenia.

By the fourth year of my extended adolescence, I was beginning to see that it would require many additional hours of school to right what I had already irreparably screwed up. I hadn't hit rock bottom in my karaoke addiction yet, so I could not see that as part of the problem. Maybe I needed a job that was less stressful? I was a secretary for an optometrist, and I had been thinking about quitting since the day I started. The office was located in a mall that time forgot, and the decor was something you'd see in dumpstered VHS pornography: brown paneling, brown scratchy industrial carpeting, brown cabinetry, and the eye doctor wore only brown or mustard polyester pantsuits from the Blair catalog. He had been contentious when I was a young patient asking for prescription 3-D glasses, and time never softened his feelings toward me. As rude as he was to me, he was twice as mean to the two middle-aged women I worked with. Between discussions about their children and the latest soaps, we conspired against the eye doctor.

"Michael decided he's going to the junior prom with Lenore," Maureen said, unwrapping a piece of chocolate, part of the endless supply the doctor kept on hand to quell any subversive ideas.

"That's terrific!" said Anna. "I wish Kyle would go to his prom."

"Let's put Ex Lax in Doc's coffee!" I suggested, sucking the innards out of a cherry cordial. It was while working at the doctor's that I realized I had a headache nearly every day. I refused to believe that it was the excessive amount of chocolate I was consuming or the stress of putting my education on indefinite hold. Instead, I attributed it to dust, aggravation, and that I could trust that everyday at 3:00 p.m., I would hear "Love Shack" on the Lite FM station that was our only contact with the outside world. What was most painful about my workday was that no one else seemed to notice the repetition.

"Guys," I said, addressing my coworkers. Anna looked up from applying cakey, tarantula mascara and Maureen stopped shoveling Rolos into her mouth. "It's 2:59. In one minute, the radio is going to play 'Love Shack.'"

For sixty seconds, we stared at each other in tense anticipation.

*"If you see a painted sign at the side of the road...!"*

"How did you do that?" Anna asked, awestruck by my power to summon motivating soft rock.

"It's like this *every day*. Every day I come here, smell old carpeting and polyester pants, and wait for 'Love Shack.' Every day is *Groundhog Day*. Is this all there is to our existence? Are we this *empty?*" I said this with pained meaning, hoping to lead Anna and Maureen to freedom like a Norma Rae of secretary ass.

Instead, each day after that, Anna and Maureen would look up from their paperwork at 3:00 p.m.

"Hey! It's your[11] song!" they would say, humming along to the Fred Schneider parts as they filled out insurance forms.

Although my job at the eye doctor involved very little personal responsibility, I felt that the dress clothes I was required to wear were somehow keeping me from completing college. I also reasoned that they were partially at fault for my headaches. I started to think about my time working at a grocery store when I was seventeen. Nothing at all was expected of me. I had long forgotten about the wish I made every day at lunchtime

---

11 There is nothing worse than hating something and then having people refer to it as "your" thing, as in, *"your* Gallagher watermelon-smashing act!" or *"your* teratoma!"

that God would cause the grocery belt to tear off my scanning hand so that I would no longer have to work or go on to college. This idea of a low-expectation job only became sweeter as my time at the optometrist's office wore on.

I applied at a natural food store one day while I was buying an organic headache remedy and feeling nostalgic for my carefree youth. To my surprise, they hired me on the spot. To celebrate, I dyed my hair neon pink and told the Doc I was never coming back.

"I'm Steve," said the man filling out my paperwork. "I'll be your Team Leader." At the natural food store, the lingo was designed around a sense that everyone was on the same Team, with the ultimate goals being Fun and Profit. My experience there has since caused me to amend my opinion on terms such as these because any company fostering a Team Atmosphere is usually Purposely Misleading and, in fact, Working for Satan.

Steve had the gray hair and hopeful outlook of someone that had probably at one point in their life traveled the country in a Volkswagen and had one or more drug-induced, same-sex experiences they would never tell their children about. He asked me what I did for fun, what kind of music I listened to, and he absorbed the answers with the same closed-eye nodding of someone ingesting an acid tab. Although only the day before I had dyed my hair bright pink, I still had no tolerance for Steve's brand of hippie bullshit.

"Alright!" he said brightly, after finishing up an anecdote about a Canned Heat show he had once attended. "Let's get down to business! For training today, you'll be working with Chandra in The Box."

Although what he was saying seemed to be intentionally clouded by secret code, I got the basic gist of it. Chandra was probably a seventeen-year-old girl, not unlike the child I once was, probably ungrateful for the easy job she now had. Perhaps I could expand her worldview by sharing my experiences of the cruelties of the real world. I was also certain The Box was slang for the customer service desk.

*"Do you party?"* Chandra would ask, using the cryptic language of the futureless. I would enlighten her, explaining that

the way of drugs is not the way of success. Then I would ride my bicycle to the Russian literature class I was taking for the second time.

Steve paged for Chandra and while we waited, I thought of how the bleach I had used on my hair was making my scalp itch. A man, about eighty years old and of Southeast Asian descent, suddenly appeared before us.

"Chandra," Steve said, addressing the prunish and feeble old man. "This is Cassie. She'll be working with you today in The Box."

Chandra nodded with the solemn acceptance of a prisoner of war.

"Since you're working in The Box, you might want to put on a sweater." Steve walked away and left me with Chandra, who nodded in agreement and scuttled toward the freezer. Quickly, it occurred to me just what The Box was.

The job of those relegated to The Box is to wait for someone to purchase a refrigerated item. Then, one must replenish that item by pushing another to the front of the freezer case or replace it altogether. Although he looked to have one foot in the grave, Chandra responded to this task with the strength and guile of Dhalsim in *Street Fighter,* hurtling gallons of organic milk as though they were empty. Frozen solid, my nose began to run and I got a crippling headache, rendering me useless to Chandra. There was a silent and persistent tension for the five hours we spent as one in The Box.

A supervisor approximately half my age poked her head inside the freezer to announce it was break time. I stepped out into the warmth of the real world and Chandra produced a pack of clove cigarettes from his pocket and stormed off. My brain was a brick of ice, and I tried desperately to remember where I had put my bag. I ran into Steve, who was pretending to fire a scanning device as though it were a ray gun.

"Looks like somebody's been in The Box!" he said, taking a playful flick at my bright red nose.

"Just how long am I going to be in this Box for?"

"The Box is a responsibility in which we all must partake."

"What?"

"We all must participate in The Box from time to time."

It was very apparent that I had made a grave mistake. I would rather suffer any fate than a slow death of brainfreeze, and I would also rather wring out the respective crotches of the polyester pants of an entire optometry school than ever go back in The Box. "Look, Steve. I get splitting migraines if I'm cold. I'm afraid The Box is no longer an option. You're gonna have to work something else out." Steve made some thoughtful noises that suggested he was thinking of an alternative and then told me to go on break.

I sat in the sun for half an hour like a gecko on a heating rock. I would have left, but my pocketbook was inside and I felt too awkward to reach around Steve to grab it and run. Plus, I had a million bills and I had told the eye doctor I hated him. I had no choice but to stick it out and freeze to death with the same cheerful resignation as the dreadlocked, vegan assholes who were now my coworkers.

When I went back inside, Steve informed me of the new game plan for my training.

"You're going to be working with Nick next." He paged Nick, but this time I did not allow my imagination to create a fantasy scenario of what I would be doing or whom I would be working with.

Nick was a seventeen-year-old boy. Our job was to gather the carts in the parking lot.

"You get that side," he said, gesturing to the end of the parking lot that was littered with thousands of carts like a prairie of grazing steer. Nick's side of the parking lot had an SUV of blonde teenage girls with a stereo bumping a Nelly song. At any job I have ever had at an establishment that necessitated shopping carts, the person whose job it was to gather them was a teenage boy or an adult who talked and sang to shopping carts.

"I am not seventeen anymore. This has got to be the lowest point of my life," I said to myself, struggling to push the carts, while twenty feet away my coworker was copping a feel and probably thinking about how awesome his life was.

Before I left that night, Nick made me lift several eighty-pound boxes of shopping bags onto a cart while he ate expired cookies from the stockroom. Then they informed me I had to work at four in the morning the next day.

"Rest up!" said Steve as he locked the door behind me.

I cried the entire drive home. Once I got home, I dug up my father's heating pad for my aching back and cried some more. It had seemed like a good idea: if I had an easier job, I could finish school in a reasonable amount of time. At no point did I factor in that years of desk jobs had made me unwilling to put up with the amount of grunt work that I had been willing to deal with as a teenager. Unable to move from the couch, I called my boyfriend and hoped I could get a few complaints in before I heard the words I Told You So.

To my surprise, Dave answered the phone on the first ring.

"I was just going to call you," he said.

"Carts...frozen...team!" I choked out words between sobs. "And I have to go back in six hours!"

"Cassie, I had a dream. We have to go to Atlantic City."

"What?"

"I took a nap and I had a dream that we went to Atlantic City, put everything we had on black, and won. We have to go there tonight."

"Dave, I have to be back there at *four in the morning*," I said, crying and rubbing Aspercreme on myself. "There's *no way*."

"Cassie, it'll be like a Bruce Springsteen song. It was totally a psychic dream." Dave had a great aunt who talked to spirits. I had never met her, but in my imagination she had long white hair like the sorceress in *Willow* and spoke to glowing orbs that kept her company.

*"I know, Cliford,"* she said. *"Millionaires!"*

"Dave, I...I can't. My back hurts and I need this job!"

"Cassie, you won't need a job *when we win*."

"This is a terrible idea," I said. Dave had stolen his father's gas card and I had taken the EZ Pass from my mother's car. I had no psychic feeling about our drive, but I was pretty sure that any karmic change of fortune did not involve petty theft.

"Cassie," he said, not taking his eyes from the road, "I'm telling you...."

Atlantic City never seemed like a place of great prosperity to me. I always associated it with my parents leaving my sister and me without food for the weekend and coming back two days later to remortgage our house. Dave felt differently though, and we listened to *Nebraska* the whole way there.

"Who the fuck is the Chickenman?" I asked.

"It doesn't matter. Just listen to the *meaning!*"

We decided on the Wild Wild West Casino when we got there. Dave had a good feeling about it and I enjoyed the chlorinated smell of the fountains when we walked in. It reminded me of Epcot Center, and I felt like if I was going to lose everything I had, it might as well be in an air of vacation-like pleasantries.

While Dave scouted around for the roulette wheel, I took a good look at the type of person that is up at two in the morning on a Tuesday in Atlantic City. They were a hardened bunch, weathered by time, nicotine, and poor financial decisions. I looked at Dave and me: soft, pasty, and sheltered by our own unwillingness to enter the real world. Both of us viewed college as a nebulous goal, a diploma an object one aspires to attain, but never actually does. Neither of us knew anyone who had actually completed college, and the few people we met who had, somehow seemed that if we kicked them when they weren't expecting it, a panel would pop off to reveal springs and an infrared device.

"It's over there," Dave said, gesturing to wheels near a sign blinking the word REDEMPTION. "It's now or never."

Combined, we only had about forty dollars.

But when we lost that forty dollars, it hurt worse than losing ten years off our lives.

"At least we have each other," I suggested on the walk back to the car that we had paid eight dollars to park.

Dave muttered unconvincingly, and we drove back home.

"I can't believe my dream lied to me," he said later, angry that the abilities of his witchy aunt had passed him over. "I was sure we were going to win."

"I just don't think we'll ever have that kind of luck, Dave."

The sun was coming up over the George Washington Bridge when I quit my job.

"Hi," I said into the phone. "My name's Cassie and I just started last night and this job really wasn't what I was expecting so I went to Atlantic City and put everything on black and lost and I'm quitting right now. I'm sorry. Bye."

We bought bagels that morning with car change. Dave turned off *Nebraska,* opting instead for early morning AM talk radio, brooding over the static hum of traffic and weather conditions. I called up the eye doctor and begged for my job back, knowing that there is no greater motivator for moving on with your life than working at a job that you hate. It took two more years of school for a piece of fancy paper I will be paying off for the rest of my life to finally confirm what I knew all along: betting on myself is the only sure thing.

## *Sweet Charity*

There were two competing charities constantly at war in the parking lot of the bookstore. The first was DARE, which I thought had been eliminated in favor of bigger prisons and sparkier means of human euthanasia, but I guess it never really went away. Instead, it was at slumber, biding its time, like Bruce Wayne taking a nap, waiting for the Penguin to be up to his old tricks again.

The people who worked for DARE were born-again in their righteous conviction to fight for drug-free youth, and their enthusiasm while turning the other cheek at the inevitable letdown when nobody cared was the emotional equivalent of Jesus smiling while being fitted for headgear: *"Miss, if you could just take a minute. We're helping out kids today. Ma'am. Sir. We're helping out kids today. Sir, we're keeping kids off the street today. Ma'am...."*

The thing about these people was that at first glance they all appeared normal, but upon closer inspection, there was one physical feature about them that set them apart from the rest of society. The main DARE representative was okay-looking in a Rick Moranis sort of way, but his glasses could best be described as the "I went to the eye doctor, and this is all my insurance would pay for" sort of glasses. The female DARE representative looked like someone who would be attractive, if not for giant, mumps-swollen cheeks, which caused her to sound like Rabbit from *Winnie the Pooh*. Anyone willing to prostitute their dignity for a pansy concept like "the good of the children" is usually unfuckable in a saintly way. Once they have achieved the Ultimate Good, they become cute in a quirky, *She's All That* sort of way, but until then, they just look like the guy on the bus who you wonder if he's touching himself or trying to stop his phone from vibrating.

The second charity that fought for control of the bookstore parking lot was called, "Kids Who Will Call You a No-Assed Bitch If You Don't Buy Their Candy." The dominating principle of this charity was to make rich people feel uncomfortable enough to purchase a five-dollar bag of M&Ms in the hope that their car would not be keyed on a return trip to buy *O'Reilly Factor For Kids*.

Although I supported entrepreneurship in its varied forms, I hated these fucking kids. I don't usually hate anyone, least of all anyone with the ability to cause guilt to come pouring out of over-privileged assholes in shows of stuttering, fearful generosity. What I did hate about these kids, aside from being loud, obnoxious, and the fact that they were clearly using this money for drugs, is *they littered.*

On a recent excursion through my mom's attic, I came across a marble notebook from when I was in the third grade. In scribbly pencil across one of the pages is written:

*ENVIRONMENT SAVER'S CLUB*
Members:
Cassie Joy Sneider, President
Carly Jane Sneider, Vice President
Mallory, Secretary
Michael, Treasurer

A predecessor to the modern-day Earth Liberation Front, our methods were considered radical by our opponents, mainly my parents, who screamed at me when I rode down the block on my bicycle, picking up garbage from the lawns of our white-trash neighbors. Although this club has since disbanded from disinterest on the parts of the other officers, I hold steadfast to its main tenant to defend Mother Nature with the fervor of Steven Seagal fighting his way out of a stranglehold. There is no worse scumbag than a litterer, and if you litter in my presence, I will make a lion-hearted effort to snap your neck in three different places.

I had a history with the candy kids that predated working at the bookstore by many years. There used to be this thing called the "Long Island music scene," which no longer exists in its original form, but has picked up and reassembled itself in Brooklyn, sort of like CBGBs in Las Vegas, but insert, "toilet where Lou Reed peed" with "losers with Jawbreaker tattoos." Eighty percent of this scene had a job at Tower Records at some point, and the other 20 percent hung out in the parking lot after hours waiting for the rest to get off work. I was in the latter category, and as such was accosted in the parking lot by these kids every time I went to visit my boyfriend. One day, we were saying goodbye when they shouted, "Get a motherfuckin' hotel!"

Tumbleweeds of cardboard emblazoned with the M&M logo blew across the parking lot. I imagined a seagull with a Snickers wrapper cutting off its oxygen supply, and something inside of me snapped.

"That's it. I'm stealing their candy."

James and Greg distracted them by walking in opposite directions and announcing they wanted candy. The kids split up and left their precious Costco packs of Starburst next to the curb. I pulled up next to them, snatched, grabbed, and threw the car into drive.

"Bitch is taking our candy!"

The kids, who ranged in age from eight to about twenty-five, threw themselves at my car like jackals lunging at a zebra. I peeled out of the parking lot and drove home, where, satisfied with myself, I ate about fifteen bags of Skittles, the wrath of whose karma can still be seen on my ass and thighs.

Time passed, and I came to the conclusion that the appearance of these peddlers with their laminated false proof of Boys and Girls Club Memberships and debate teams was an insulated phenomenon, something only the employees of Tower Records were meant to suffer through, like a modern day Sodom and Gomorrah.

"'Scuse me ma'am. Would you like to buy some candy to help out my basketball team?" Shortly after I started working at the bookstore, I realized that abject poverty among adolescent basketball teams was spreading on a global scale.

"No, I wouldn't. Our store has a no solicitation policy, so you're gonna have to find someplace else to go." I said this with a twinge of optimism, as though I was offering him a choice.

"I ain't goin' nowhere," said the kid, who was at most thirteen years old.

"Look, kid. I don't want to fight with you. I'm only following store policy, so just find another parking lot. There's a mall right across the street." I gestured to the mall's parking lot, which was about two hundred feet away. I was extending the olive branch with an array of options. How could anyone argue when presented with such a reasonable alternative?

"I ain't goin' nowhere," the kid said again, defiantly throwing down his candy. He had marked his territory, not knowing that he was barking up a tree that doesn't fuck around.

"Well, then I'm gonna have to call the police."

"Whateva. I ain't goin' nowhere. You think you can mess with me, you got anotha thing comin.'"

"Well, then I'm gonna go inside and call the police and you can sit out here with your candy and wait for them." I turned to walk in the building, impressed by how calm I was remaining. This was a new Cassie, one that was not so quick to act with theft or violence. Perhaps the years had wizened me and I had turned over a new leaf.

"Bitch, I ain't goin' *nowhere*."

*A bolt of lightning strikes the roof of Dr. Frankenstein's laboratory. It electrifies the metal rods connected to the monster's neck, reanimating the abnormal brain. Its eyes flutter, and as the chains strapping him to the gurney snap, one thing is for certain: all hell is about to break loose.*

"What did you say?"

"I said, 'I ain't goin' *nowhere, Bitch.*' Now whachu gonna do about it?" He folded his arms, indicating that no, I probably was not going to do anything about it. Then I realized that he thought I was some kind of Dana Plato, made-for-TV adult, certainly not someone with twenty-three years of angst and Ace Frehley guitar-solos flooding into her phantom balls.

"Take it back."

"No."

"Take it back."

"Make me. *Bitch.*"

Some women embrace the notion of Bitch. They wear key chains that say so alongside ones that declare why chocolate is better than men. These women have an inner sadness about them, one that causes them to watch *Friends* in syndication and tape pictures of Johnny Depp to their cubicles. Bitch is a pink baby doll tee worn by someone with flabby arms. Bitch is a license plate on a car bought with an alimony check. *Bitch* is a magazine that has rejected me numerous times.

I am a lot of things, and Psycho is more like it.

I kicked the box of candy like Pele scoring a winning field goal in the World Cup of Life. It rained down upon the parking lot in the bite-sized rainbow dreams of a fat kid.

"You kicked my candy, *Bitch!*"

Cars backed up, pulling in and out of the parking lot, crushing creamy nougat centers into real fruit flavors.

I walked inside.

"You kicked my motherfuckin' candy, Bitch!" The kid chased me up to the entrance of the building, where one of the other managers had seen the whole thing.

"Whoa, whoa, whoa. What's going on here?" she asked, even though she was witness to my victory punt.

"Bitch kicked my candy! Bitch kicked my *candy!*"

"Did you kick his candy?" she asked, merely as a formality before dismissing him.

"I have no idea what he's talking about."

"That's a *lie!* She *kicked* my *candy!* Bitch kicked my candy!" He screamed as though he was caught in a bear trap, spittle flying in every which direction. For a second, his dramatic portrayal of being a victim made me uncertain of my own scot-free getaway. Maybe I would get written up for this. The week before I had gone to work with a black eye. Perhaps someone had ratted that I had gotten it at the MAC counter of Macy's and not in a bar fight with a chair, which was the story I told most of my coworkers while rubbing my fake purple eye. I didn't expect to be employed there for much longer. It was sort of the equivalent of skating on ice you had made thin yourself by running a hairdryer on it.

When I turned around, the store manager was behind me. She was a terrifying human being, as any more than ten years of retail experience has a tendency to do to a person. She began screaming at him to leave the premises, and, much like a baby chimp running into the arms of Diane Fossey, I knew I was safe.

That day only made the cultural gap between us and them into something of a fault line. Every interaction after that was extremely volatile, threatening to turn our workplace into the scene in *The Land Before Time* when the earth splits in two. In their childlike innocence, the DARE people began setting up outside the store directly opposing the candy kids. As an English major, I seemed to be the only one on staff who appreciated good juxtapositioning when I saw it.

"Cassie, can you call the cops?"

"Why?"

"The candy kids just threatened to kill the DARE lady."

There doesn't seem to be much of a payoff in charity work, which is part of the reason why I quit Girl Scouts when I was seven. Even as a child, I knew that in the real world, most good deeds go unnoticed. There is no merit badge for blood, sweat, and tears, but that doesn't seem to faze the people who work for DARE. They brave the elements day after day, selling themselves for what is probably the one thing they have left to believe in.

I once made the mistake of asking the DARE guy what the point was. I got a soliloquy worthy of a Shakespearean tragedy.

"I do it for the kids," he answered, cleaning the lenses of his giant glasses on his shirtsleeve. "Yeah, most people don't want to hear about the drug epidemic, let alone donate money to put an end to it. But the drug epidemic isn't pretty, and although it's grueling work, someone has to do it. *Someone* has to protect the children."

I had always thought that the actuality of the drug epidemic was a few bored teenagers smoking weed behind a garage, but apparently I was wrong. America was facing a full-out *Land of the Dead*-style plague. Each day there were eight year-olds dying by the thousands, choking on their own vomit in basement meth labs. Soon, all of Generation X would be wiped out and replaced by Generation Y Don't You Stop Spending All of Your Money on Wall Tapestries of Jim Morrison, Cut Your Fucking Dreads, and Get a Job?

I believe that most people are, at their very core, just as selfish and charred as I am. Gandhi went on a hunger strike because he wanted hips like Nicole Ritchie, Clara Barton had a thing for amputees, Joan of Arc was a pyromaniac, and Mother Theresa liked to pick scabs. Perhaps he was doing it for the satisfaction of being able to beat off at the end of the day to the mental images of all those drug-free children, because no person is willing to endure that sort of punishment for the good of society.

Some people find it hard to believe that I am not a regular drug user. This is something I don't understand, considering that I bathe regularly, hate jam bands, and would rather gouge out my own eyes than wear sandals in public. I used to think that fun was my anti-drug, but upon further consideration, I suppose I was wrong. Total judgment of anyone different than me is my anti-drug. Eventually, when I am in jail for beating the shit out of someone for wearing a sweatshirt made of hemp with a dancing bear on it, maybe Jesus and forgiveness will become my anti-drug. But as long as there are ducks covered in oil, choking on fundraiser packs of Twizzlers, *somebody* has to save them from this garbage-strewn earth.

And that someone is this bitch right here.

# Creep

"Being *creepy* is just temporary." Alyssa turned the wheel, slowly navigating the Jeep forward through the darkened end of the parking lot.

"Like, 'dabbling' in creepiness?" I suggested, looking out the window at the cars slowing down to thoughtfully size up the other drivers. It was only 10:30 p.m., on the early side for seeing anything really disturbing.

"Exactly. Like, what we're doing right now is creep*y*, but it doesn't make us *creeps*."

"But if we did it every day, it would," I offered.

"Right." We parked in a space with a good vantage point and turned off the headlights. I took a sip of 7-Eleven coffee and placed it in the cup holder. The radio played the Eagles softly. "Like Spongebob Guy. Now *that's* a creep."

With Spongebob Guy, Alyssa and Colin had made me do all the talking. He had a head of tight, brown curls, wore brown plastic aviators, and drove a brown Toyota Corolla. It was as if the color was bleached from his life, leaving everything a sun-faded umber. He had his chubby white arm stuck out the window, begging companionship.

"You do it!" Colin and Alyssa said.

"Why do I have to do it?" It was my first time visiting the Park and Ride. I did not see why that meant I was the most eligible candidate to spark up a conversation.

"You're a good talker," said Alyssa.

"Plus, you're driving, so you can react more quickly if stuff gets weird," Colin added.

"C'mon, guys! I hate this!"

"You're the only one of us who can do it."

I pulled up next to the car. "Uh, hey fella," I said.

"H-hey," he said, already so nervous he was sweating. He was overweight, and the buttons on his salmon-colored shirt were separating, leaving taut folds of pulled skin.

Colin elbowed me. "Uh, so what are you into?" I asked.

"Y-you know. Little of everything. I come here to watch."

"Uh-huh," I responded. My eyes darted to the composting bags of Wendy's in the backseat and then to the stickers stuck willy-nilly all over the back window. "Uh, so, you're into Spongebob?" I pointed plaintively at the sticker-job.

A look of guilt washed over his face. "Th-those belong to my kids." We looked each other in the eyes for a shameful, perverse moment. He fumbled with the shifter and peeled out of the parking lot.

Colin and Greg cheered from the backseat. "Guys, that was gross. I'm not talking to anybody else."

"Did you see the remorse in his eyes?" Alyssa said through laughter-induced tears.

"Dude, that was somebody's *dad!* Somebody's DAD just came here with the intent of watching somebody *else's* dad get it on. What is wrong with Long Island? And why are *we* here?"

Colin spoke up. "We don't have anything better to do."

When I was growing up, my mother would shoo me out of the living room, urging me to find something better to do. I would then drag myself up the stairs to my room, dejectedly lying spread out on the floor, staring up at a purple unicorn poster for inspiration. I usually settled for making puppets out of my socks or taping Steppenwolf off of the radio. Sometimes I would go outside and take every earthworm I found and put them in the same coffee can to set them free as a group. The things I did never seemed much better than being inside, staring at my mother while she painted her toenails or watched *Oprah*. I guess I just always assumed that one day, I would know what the better thing I was supposed to be doing was and go do it.

People my age are married. I have attended their weddings and showers, scratching my head in bewilderment. I never understood how people get where they are going with such certainty, a steadfastness that allows them to commit to relationships and large pieces of furniture and jobs that have

401(k)s. They have kids and those kids have karate and soccer practice, and they are caught in an endless loop of responsibility, like a broken 8-track playing "Freebird" at half-speed. It is too much for me to wrap my brain around, but I dutifully attend milestone functions anyway, congratulating people for things I would rather have a lifetime of cold sores than ever to be anchored with myself.

There is a long list of things I can't be bothered with, and that list is wrapped in a list of things I would rather do. Both are endless scrolls of double-ply toilet paper, bouncing and rolling on forever, absorbing time-filling activities, conversations with strangers, and the feeling of a car rolling over miles and miles of asphalt. I have been around for twenty-something years, and it has never occurred to me how I should better occupy my time. I am feeling my way around in the dark, and I am bumping into my closest friends as we crawl around the same meaningless cave.

I dialed Alyssa's number and waited, looking directly into the gray eyes of the straggly-haired old man on the monitor.

"Yeah?"

"So, like, remember when you told me I should look at the Sex Offender Database because you bet me there was a ton of sex offenders in Ronkonkoma? Well, in junior high, there was this house we used to pass on the bus with all these security cameras outside and people would say it was Pester the Molester's house."

"Uh-huh."

"Well, his last name really is Pesta. Like, with an 'a.' Isn't that crazy?"

"Those are pretty incredible odds."

"I know! It's, like, totally which came first, you know?"

"Yeah, that's pretty weird."

"Well, I'll let you go. I just wanted to tell you."

"Okay. Call me tomorrow."

"Okay. Bye!"

"You oughtta get a civil service job. Take the test, you'll be outta there in twenty years, with benefits." My cousin works for the county. In the hall of his house, there is a picture of our family gathered around him on the day he graduated from the academy. I am fourteen, chubby, wearing a blue leopard-print dress with my hair hanging in my eyes. He is young, smiling, and his hair is not all-white, like it is now.

"Uh, I dunno. I've thought about it, but I kind of feel like I have a better chance of doing the awesome things I really want to do now without having a job that is killing me."

"You're twenty-seven. Thirty's not too far away, and when it comes, man...." He trailed off, leaving me to imagine the apocalyptic scenario of me turning thirty without gainful employment. Truthfully, I had thought about my thirtieth birthday. December thirteenth in the year 2012 is, according to Nostradamus and the Mayans, the day after the end of the world. Brimstone and hellfire seems to dwarf any economic problems I may be having then, and I have already begun drafting a letter to Ted Nugent and Steve Buscemi, who share my birthday, inviting them to celebrate Doomsday with me. I would rather be playing in a ballpit at McDonald's or fighting the good forces of the Rapture with "Stranglehold" playing on unseen speakers, instead of worrying about my retirement funds.

I say this, but I don't think anyone imagines being old. There is no way Debbie Harry was thinking about varicose veins when she was fucking Clem Burke on a ripped leather couch in the back room of CBGBs. My cousin probably did not imagine he would have a head of white hair, and I never imagined, as the eighth-grader in that picture, that it all wouldn't have fallen into place by now. You can die young and stay pretty, as the song says, but most of us end up where we are going no matter what. You can fight it, or you can give into it, and the result is usually the same, the same gravity bearing down on everyone, rolling us down and out like souvenir pennies.

I took Peter to the Park and Ride once.

"I'll do the talking. We kind of just have to bait ourselves and then they'll start coming over to check us out."

Peter reached for the bag of gummy bears. "This is seriously creepy." He said it in a glad way, then picked out three orange bears and ate them.

We weren't parked long before a station wagon pulled up alongside us. The driver had a graying white-guy afro and a polo shirt. He smiled. We smiled back. A round of pleasant head-nods.

"Uh, hey," I began. "How's it going?"

"Pretty good. Just checkin' out the scene."

"Uh-huh," I said, nodding. "Ya like what ya see?"

Peter started to laugh. I grabbed his hand and squeezed it.

"What's a young, attractive couple like you doing at a place like this?" He gestured to the dark parking lot, headlights beaming in slow, pathetic circles.

"We're swingers," I answered, quickly. "We're just…" Peter laughed and covered it up with a cough, "looking for a good time."

"WELL," the man said, "let me tell you something. I am the CEO of a marketing company. All of my employee's health records pass through me, and I know for a fact that most of my employees are in the swinging lifestyle and every last one has contracted a disease in the last year."

Peter squeezed my hand.

"Play it cool, Cassie," I thought.

"So if you think you are safe and having a 'carefree' time, you had best wrap it up." He turned suddenly wistful. "I used to swing. Oh, yes. I've cheated on my wife. I've brought home a few bugs, but thank the lord she's taken me back. Now I just come here to watch. I get my excitement that way. It's the only way that's truly safe."

Peter dropped the gummy bears on the floor. We were both staring, openmouthed. This was reality. Peter squeezed my hand again, and the three of us looked off toward the headlights driving in circles, a game of flashlight tag where everyone wins.

*Things I Wanted To Be When I Grew Up*
1. mad scientist
2. cowboy
3. starving artist
4. runway model
5. writer

I guess I'm not doing so bad.

★

I spend a lot of time trying to one-up myself with brain candy, but in the future, I would like to learn how to crochet. It seems like an activity where I might be able to shut myself down for a few minutes, listening to words speak out of the television and letting them wash over me like waves in a pool. My mother is especially good at crosswords, but they are just too cerebral for the kind of leisure I want. I want to feel brain-damaged and vegetative.

Alyssa and I have had an ongoing discussion about the difference between being a creep and just being creepy.

"I kind of feel like there are no checks and balances," I said, adjusting my seat belt.

"What do you mean?"

"Like, if I were to call up you, or Colin, or anyone else I really care about and said, 'Dude, I just watched someone take a dump on a piece of Plexiglas,' you would say, 'Cool! I'm making chili. Want to come over?'"

"I see," she said.

"Like, how are we going to know when we crossed over and we've gone from being creepy into being full-blown creeps?"

Alyssa thought for a moment. "Maybe it's like when you get your first period and you just kind of know it."

"Like, I'll ask to go to the bathroom and see that I'm finally a creep?"

"Exactly. Because someone will be there to watch you."

Alyssa fixed her eyeliner in the rearview. The marshmallows in my coffee had cooled to a gelatinous chemical, sticking to the lid of the cup. I scooped them out with my finger, a monkey stirring the ant pile, and I thought I was pretty lucky to know so many people with nothing better to do.

## *Picture Book*

The room was lit by candles and dimmed by smoke that filled bars in the days before laws banned cigarettes to the outer layers of space. The songbooks on the tables read as testaments to the fickleness of twentieth century popular music: here-today, gone-tomorrow songs from a time when you could still buy Top 40 singles at the mall. There were a handful of regulars at the bar, some stabbing the ice in their glasses, hoping for water to reanimate the stagnant alcohol, others flipping though the white binders of pre-recorded song titles. We were all waiting for something to happen, for the crackle of the speakers to ignite the air of the basement of the Comfort Inn with a lifespark that even I, in my teen thirst for irony, needed. There was an unspoken sadness in being a regular on a Tuesday night at the Gateway Lounge, but it was a sadness that when you held it up to the neon disco lights casting shadows on the small stage, you could *see right through it.*

"You have to come tonight!" Colin was dumping chemicals from the negative developer into a bucket. We would then bring the bucket out behind Kmart, dump it into an even larger 55-gallon drum, and watch the toxic liquids overflow onto a patch of dead grass. Although working at Kmart should have registered on my radar as humiliating and beneath me, I was able to write off all the film I was taking as corporate waste. It was actually costing the company more to have me on board than the $7.50 an hour they decided my time as a Photo Lab Technician was worth. The red vest I had to wear was a small price to pay for all the nude photos of other people Colin and I were pocketing. Our favorite was the roll of small children at a petting zoo, topped off by a Kodak moment of a morbidly obese woman in a bathtub, spattered in finger-paint with a fistful of cotton swabs sticking out of her vagina like some sort of gynecological *Hellraiser*.

"I don't know, dude," I said, scenes of a retirement party flashing on the screen in rapid succession. "I've never sung in front of people before, and I don't know how into public embarrassment I am."

"Me and Tom went last week," Colin said, hefting the bucket into a shopping cart. "The DJ ripped off his shirt during 'Dream On' and there was this duo of horse-faced twentysomethings singing 'Love Shack' like it was their *fucking job*. You have to go."

"Maybe." It wasn't true that I had never sung in public before. My band, the Genetically-Altered Squirrels, formed for the sole purpose of trying out for the high school talent show. After thirty seconds of confused, dissonant noise, the judges and student body lost interest in the sideshow playing in front of them, and I stood there, voice cracking and frozen with crippling adolescent fear. That day, I made a promise to myself that I would never sing in public again. I was the Elephant Man of song, and my vow of silence was a burlap sack with a crude eyehole, shielding the world from the ugliness of my voice.

But maybe I was wrong. From the moment I discovered my stepdad's cassette of *Toys in the Attic* when I was eleven and heard the first pulsing note, a voice appeared in my head. It was soft at first, a mere hum compared to the voices that screamed "PLAYING WITH REALISTIC TOY HORSES IS OKAY!" and, "MAYBE TODAY A BOY WILL KISS ME!"

Slowly, as the posters of unicorns in my room were replaced by posters of Bono, the voice grew more powerful until I could clearly discern its message: "CASSIE, YOU HAVE TO ROCK," it commanded in the wavering scream of Bruce Dickinson.

Even after my humiliation at the Talent Show, the voice maintained a dull, persistent roar in my ears. In spite of my fear of failure, and in spite of the fact that I had no musical talent whatsoever, I knew deep down that I had been chosen to rock. Although certainly not the day I stood shivering before an auditorium of my peers, but someday.

Somewhere in the void of my soul that had been so deformed and poisoned by rock and roll music, I wanted to sit upright without asphyxiating on the hideousness of my shame, tear the twiney rope that hid my singing voice from the world, feel the spotlight on my misshapen face, and sing, loudly, proudly, "Run to the hills. Run for your lives."

I wanted to *rock*.

I passed the Gateway Lounge often, usually on the way to the Country Kitchen franchise Colin and I frequented because the night manager looked like Michael Douglas in *Falling Down*. Actually, the only ingredient it took for us to become regulars anywhere was a waiter who resembled a C-list celebrity, or the malignant smog of Section 8 desperation choking inside it.

The one indication of nightlife occurring in the basement of the hotel that housed the Gateway was the sign chasing the letters C-O-C-K in green neon. The TAILS portion had long ago shorted out and now made only a sickly buzzing sound audible if you got close enough. The hotel was located just off of the Long Island Expressway on a polluted main drag that offered car dealerships, adult shops, and the DMV. It also had weekly rates, so the crowd that gathered at the bar to sing over instrumental Billy Joel needed only unplug the hot plate they were cooking on, throw on some slippers, and venture downstairs.

I got off work at Kmart and went home to shower away the residue of photo chemicals and white-trash consumerism. Karaoke that night seemed to fall into the category of Vague Plans I Make That I Have No Intention of Following Through With. Ninety percent of the time I say, "Hell yeah, I'll be there!" I end up in my room listening to Van Halen and rubbing one out.

For most of my life I have experienced an everyday crippling social anxiety. I was shy as a child, which turned to "awkward" and then eventually "unfuckable" as I got older. I was the kid who turns bright red when they are called on in class and goes home to make detailed 1:18-scale models of dinosaurs in their room, humming along with the radio to drown out the sound of a parental screaming match. If I were a boy, I probably would have ended up with an addiction to scat porn and a degree in computer science. Instead, I didn't date anyone until I was eighteen and still make occasional references to Randy Rhodes that nobody gets. Although I would consider myself unscathed in the Shyness Scale of Animal Torturer to a Dell Customer Service Representative, it has been an uphill struggle to make it to the point where I don't want to cry when a stranger tries to talk to me.

Sometime around my sophomore year, I realized that my shyness wasn't getting me anywhere. The teachers I had all looked like out-of-work character actors. My chemistry teacher had a Freddie Mercury at Live Aid moustache and a knack for accidentally setting himself on fire. Several times while demonstrating the instability of certain elements, he burned himself, textbooks, and his desk. One day, Mr. Costello was trying to explain that potassium was a highly volatile element. I was chuckling to myself so hard that he asked me to share with the class what was so funny.

"If potassium is so volatile, how come monkeys aren't exploding out of the trees from the amount of potassium in bananas?"

I had never spoken in school before. I always imagined that if I did, everyone would make fun of me and it would turn into the video for "Jeremy." Instead, the class chuckled, and though my sense of humor has evolved to a place where I now know that that was *not funny at all,* for the first time in my young life, I felt cool. Realizing the power of my awesome joke, Mr. Costello was both incensed and flabbergasted. He produced a large metal cone. The class looked on in horror as, sweating and shaking, he sprinkled a dusting of potassium in it, lit a match, and caused a white ball of flame to almost wipe out a student in the front row.

"You almost killed Dan," I said. "Shouldn't we be practicing safety in the lab?" I was off to a great start in my new life as an extrovert, but I lacked the confidence to show the world all of the terrible jokes I was thinking.

When my friends went away to college, I chose a close-to-home state school. I wasn't sure that I had the viable social skills one needed in order to avoid becoming one of those people who has a nervous breakdown in their first semester and returns home to spend the rest of their life watching professional wrestling, swatting away flies when they land on the tower of pizza boxes in front of the TV. My first semester of college was pretty lonely and the only friend I made was the kid with green hair who worked at the video store down the block.

"Do you have *Chopping Mall?*" It was a Friday night and I had an armful of VHS.

"Dude, somebody just rented that one," said Victor, the store clerk.

"Alright, how about *Sleepaway Camp?*"

"Nah, but that movie is sick."

"I know. I saw it at a sleepover in junior high and everyone screamed at the ending."

"Classic. *Clah-sick!*" For months, my most meaningful human interactions involved deconstructing the gore scenes of slasher films with Victor. Somehow in that time, I started dating someone, and it turned out that he was friends with Victor, too. What I didn't know in my months of watching *Leprechaun in the Hood* and *Troll 2* by myself was that there was an underworld of people who didn't go away to school. Instead, they hung out in video and record stores and all-night diners and basements and garages. They talked about how the underwater shark-fight scene in *Zombie* is the greatest cinematic moment of all time. They thought of names for bands that practiced once and broke up. They drank coffee and got high and failed classes and moved to the city and hopped trains and went vegan and made out. They had crappy part-time jobs and big dreams and formed a living, breathing organism of people who spit in your food and stole your street signs and would never ever turn thirty.

I met Colin because he was running the record label that was recording my boyfriend's band. He needed someone to book shows and make posters, and at the time, I was between jobs. Actually, I had quit my job at the grocery store for the second year in a row because I didn't want to work on my birthday, which I felt was an insult to my strict punk rock ethos and eventual life goal of being true to myself until death. I felt like greener pastures were right around the corner, so instead of requesting the day off, I quit.

Colin was the manager of the Photo Lab at Kmart and he got me the job there. It took two applications, because on the first one where it asked for Alternate Means of Contact, I had written "SMOKE SIGNALS, TELEPATHY, GIANT GONG." This didn't go over well with Lynda, the human resources secretary, and Colin had to beg them to hire me.

The best part of any job is watching the orientation videos. This is where, as the newly hired, you can guess what the company has been sued for in the past. My guess was that Kmart had had a few attempts at reform and unionization, probably by idealistic comrades in arms forced into less-than-satisfactory part-time employment by staggered community college scheduling, nagging parents, and recreational drug habits. The anti-union video at Kmart is known to few, but the dramatic highs and lows rival that of zombie-versus-shark among the slacker film critics that have been exposed to it. In it, Joe Employee has everything going for him until he tries to start a union at Kmart. Then he loses his job. He can't keep up with the mortgage payments, and his wife and kids take off after the house goes into foreclosure. All his dreams are essentially crushed because he wanted better health benefits and protection from unfair hiring practices.

"You see the videos yet?" Colin asked. It was break time at my first day on the job.

"Yeah, dude. All that because of unions. Does anyone take those videos seriously?"

"No way. I plan on stealing them before I leave, though."

Colin was my immediate supervisor, which meant that I had free reign to do what I wanted. We made craft projects out of the empty rolls of photo paper and overexposed the film of rude customers. Also, for some reason, the photo department had an outside phone line under the counter that no one noticed. In the days before cell phones, Colin and I used it as our own personal hotline to each other. After Colin invited me to karaoke that day, he dialed the secret line every hour to remind me not to flake out.

But that night, when it was only ten o'clock and I was in my pajamas doing David Lee Roth leg kicks in the mirror, something just didn't feel right. It seemed wrong to lie more than once and say you'd be someplace where you had no intention of going, especially when I had so much rock and roll coursing through my veins going to waste before an audience of stuffed animals. In our time together at Kmart, Colin had become my best friend. Surely he wouldn't invite me somewhere just to throw me to the wolves.

I snatched *Diver Down* where it was still spinning on the CD player, threw on a pair of pants, and grabbed my keys.

"You made it!"

The stucco walls combined with the thick smoke to create the feeling of being inside of a cancer-ridden lung. It was a wonder anyone could breathe, let alone sing, but at the candlelit tables, people were pouring over the lists of available songs.

"Yeah, you know. Wouldn't miss this for the world."

Colin's friends were different from Victor and the

underachievers I was now used to hanging out with, who were kids in tight pants and Ramones shirts who slapped my boyfriend on the back after shows, smuggled beer into all-ages venues, and drank in garages after the show when their intoxication level wasn't good enough. Colin's friends were more like me: indoor kids who liked good music and Nintendo. They wore shirts of ska bands and khaki pants and made no apologies for it. I felt more comfortable with them than I did with the other crowd. There was a lot of fashion show posturing that went along with the music and general air of irresponsibility. Leather jackets with spikes and studs were expensive, and I knew I couldn't afford them on Kmart pay.

"Cassie, this is Greg, Brian, Hoostin, Dennis, and you already know Tom. Guys, this is Cassie. She's the one who made a spear out of a cardboard tube at work, labeled it 'Spear For Annoying Customers,' and got us both in trouble."

"Awesome!" Colin's friends cheered and I knew I was in. Colin nudged a songbook in my direction. I flipped through the laminated pages and tried to discern the titles in the low light.

"So how does this work here?" I asked, squinting in the dark.

"You write your name and the song on a piece of paper and give it to the DJ. He eventually calls you up, and then you embarrass yourself. If you want drinks, the bar is up there. They card, though."

"Oh, I don't drink."

"Me either. None of us do." He pointed to the other tables of potential singers. "They do, though. And when they get trashed, it's awesome."

Usually, low light provides a soft glow capable of hiding flaws, but for some reason, acne-scarring, striations, and general creature features were still visible at the tables surrounding us. The hard-life faces of the women were caked in foundation, and the men looked, for the most part, like autopsy photos of John Wayne. There were many variations of tan, from sun-kissed Teamster to extra-crispy barmaid.

"Did you meet DJ Frankie yet?" Colin asked.

The speakers crackled, and a voiced pounded from the amps hidden beneath tacky disco lights.

*"Alriiiggght!* Thank you, Marianne! Next up to the stage–*uh-oh!* We got a special guest for you tonight. Next up is the

*ultimate*, the *fierce*, the *charismatic* one: Mister *Coliiin!* Can you come up on the stage to rock us with some *Pat Benetaaaar?"*

Colin gestured to himself, as if he were both humbled and flattered to be the recipient of such accolades. He scooted his chair back and took the stage, double-fisting the microphone and commanding the attention of the bar with the magnificent fluorescence of the ugliest Hawaiian shirt I had ever seen. His singing voice seemed actually to loosen the bowels of the people at the bar, and several of them got up to go to the bathroom. When the pre-recorded music ended, Colin gave the air a victory punch.

Our table cheered. The rest of the bar was silent.

*"Alriiight!"* said DJ Frankie, who had the vocal presence of a ham radio shut-in. "Thank you, *Coliiinn!* Now, we got a very special guest for all of you *toniiigght."* The lights dimmed to foreshadow the blinding greatness we were about to be graced with and the theme from *2001: A Space Odyssey* began to play. "Can I have to the stage the ONE. The ONLY. THE Mister. Tommy. *FLAIR!"*

I had known Tom since the eighth grade. His look could be described as Classic Nerd: a uniform of aviators, pleated khakis, and polo shirts. Tom has actually said that he wanted people to be able to recognize him from his junior high yearbook picture. He lives for old video game systems, computer programming and Hulk Hogan. But that moment, Tom stood up and moved to the stage with a swagger that was so regal it could only have come from the very essence of his soul. He held the microphone, and the transformation was complete. In that moment, he *was* Tom Jones, and his rendition of "What's New Pussycat?" could soak the panties right off of the fabled Delilah.

Everyone cheered. Me. Colin. The alcoholics at the bar. The guy in the corner with the creeping piss stain.

I scratched my song selection onto a square of paper. "Okay. I'm ready. Now what?"

"Hold on. I'll walk you up." Colin sucked the cherry out of his Sprite, and we walked to the DJ booth. DJ Frankie was invisible behind a fireworks display of party-lights. He was the great and powerful Oz behind the night's entertainment.

"Hey, Frankie. This is my friend Cassie." DJ Frankie was about forty-five. His black hair was receding and he was wearing a Hawaiian shirt that was just as ugly as Colin's.

"Why, helloooo!" he said with a Bette Davis affectation to his voice, diverting his attention from the cowboy singing "Desperado." He grabbed my hand and kissed it.

"Nice to meet you, Frankie," I said, handing him the paper.

"OH!" Frankie said, looking down at my song choice. "Greeeat song. Excellent choice. YOU are my new favorite." He winked and Colin and I walked back to the table.

"He wants to fuck you," Colin said as we took our seats.

The mic crackled. Frankie's voice echoed powerfully to life. "Ladies and gentlemen, I want you to stop what you're doing. Just *stop*, cuz whatever it is BLASPHEMY because we are about to have the sweetest angel of karaoke on stage right now. Will my *sweeeet* angel CASSIE please bring her gossamer wings to the microphone?"

Right then, right there, I knew that I had made a big mistake. It was one thing to sing in your room where there is no one to throw the olives from their watered-down martinis at you in judgment. It is quite another to inflict yourself on a hotel basement of strangers.

I hadn't opened my mouth and I was already frozen in fear.

I moved to the stage, and after that is only a self-defense memory aneurysm of a strobe light and my reflection in the fly's eye mirrors of the disco ball. I had chosen "Roxanne" by the Police, a song I did not realize while singing in the vocal fortress of my car was about twelve octaves too high. In my shit-faint panic while I croaked out the words, "You don't have to put on the red light," over and over again, I understood something rock critics have overlooked for years: Sting has no testicles. The singles "Can't Stand Losing You" and "I'm So Happy I Can't Stop Crying" are actually about his testicles. This also explains the total absence of balls in anything he has done since collaborating on "Money For Nothing."

I have a low vocal register. Monotone, really. My vocal range is consistent from waking up to going to bed at night, with the only variation occurring in instances of road rage. On the stage that night in front of Colin, my new friends, and a room of drunken strangers, I realized something: I was the one who had Sting's balls all along.

Even though I was terrified and felt that I was going to have a heart attack from the fear of being in front of a crowd, I used every rock move I had seen on MTV since birth. This included the Heart Clutch, the Reach Up, the Pull Down, the 'Oh, No You Didn't' Finger Wag, and probably a few kicks for posterity's sake. I blindly took my seat, drank a Sprite, and let the adrenaline rush through my failing heart.

"God *DAMN!*" boomed the voice through the darkness. "We have got a new nickname *toniiigght*, people! Can I please get some applause for the *Queen* of the Performance Artists, Miss *Casssiiie!*"

Music had always helped me feel more comfortable in my own skin. As long as I had a Steppenwolf tape and a mirror to sing into, I was okay. It didn't matter what things were like at home, if I wanted to melt into the floor at school and dissolve like a bad experiment in a chemistry lab. There was something in me that switched on to rock and roll, maybe because it was born of the same shyness and alienation and friction that I felt. Despite my terrible singing voice, I had rocked. The ringing in my ears began to fade, and I could hear that people were cheering and not jamming stirrers in their ears.

"Dude, that was fucking awesome!" Colin said and slapped me on the back.

"I was shaking. Is everyone deaf? That was totally shitty."

"Who cares?" he said, opening a white binder labeled BY ARTIST and shoveling a handful of salty bar pretzels into his mouth.

And maybe that was the point.

# *Homegrown*

*There is something magical about the 70s soft rock that plays over Long Island in an invisible cross-stitch, the harmless lull of xylophones a dull tenderness reminding you that maybe life's not so bad. If The Captain and Tennille, Elton and Kiki, or any of those soft rockin' power duos could exist in perfect, sexless harmony, then maybe your recent breakup and the subsequent shattering of your life are not so bad. You'll work it out. C'mon.*

They just don't make classic rock radio like they do in the free states, and on my drive home to New York, I was indescribably excited when I was able to catch the static-y tail end of "We're Not Gonna Take it" somewhere near the middle of Pennsylvania.

"Fuck yeah, East Coast!" I said, pounding the steering wheel. "We are NOT gonna take it!" I, at the moment, was one with Dee Snider, though I have always felt a bit more at one with Dee Snider than most, because we are both from Long Island and share a similar last name. The radio got clearer as I neared home, and more classic rock stations began to pop up, like an audible game of Whack-a-Mole. We were closing in on the mother lode. Blue Oyster Cult. Ratt. Sabbath. I heard them all with a steadily increasing clarity as we approached Lake Ronkonkoma, a town where it is still 1981.

Maybe the fact that I have grown up in the land that time forgot has contributed to the disconnect I feel with most people my own age. It is kind of like an itch, or a throat tickle, this feeling. I never got an iPod because I have always been able to turn on the radio with a fair chance of hearing the Van Halen version of "Pretty Woman" on any one of five classic rock stations. Those are good odds, and I feel safe here, in my car on the Long Island Expressway, returning home with all of my worldly possessions packed tightly in the trunk. I am lucky in a way, like that guy at the horse track, leaning over the railing, wearing lucky socks and lucky everything, smelling of old luck and hard times. I've got my dog in the car, and I'm coming home to where I live one block from the record store. "It's The End of the World As We Know It" is playing on the radio. Like I said, good odds.

I've toyed with the idea of satellite radio, but it just seems like cheating. Radio is not given; it is earned. The feeling of accidentally tuning in to your most favorite song in the world is unbeatable, and I guess I never lost my appreciation for the radio in its purest form, commercials and all. From 1991 until 2000, my parents drove a 1986 Buick Regal whose faculties as a car steadily eroded in its fifteen years of use. Though it came equipped with a factory AM/FM tape deck, the cassette player never worked, and after only a few weeks of owning it, someone broke off the antenna while my mother was in a store buying cigarettes.

"I came out and some sonofabitch took it," she said, sparking a Basic Ultra Light while we all stood dumbfounded around the car, like the cast of *CSI: White Trash*.

"Looks like they snapped it off," my stepfather made an educated guess, feeling the jagged nubbin of metal where the antenna once was.

"Are we gonna get another one?" my sister, Carly, and I asked. That was our main concern. Would we be able to hear C+C Music Factory on the Top 40 station? Would we again hear the careless whisper of George Michael telling us to have faith?

My parents did not answer. Instead, they went inside to stew in the juices of their misfortune, speaking only to mutter the word "sonofabitch" and to ask if we wanted Burger King for dinner.

I had a radio in my room, but a car stereo seemed necessary for the times when my parents would take us on long rides to do boring things, driving for what seemed like hours or days to look at tile and carpet samples.

"Can we try the radio?" one of us would ask. Then they would turn it on for the serenade of white noise.

"Can we *please* get an antenna?" we would ask.

"They're expensive, and I'd have to rewire a bunch of stuff in the car, and I sure as hell don't have time for that."

"What if we went to the junkyard?" Usually I would be the

one to venture into the No Man's Land territory of suggesting a step in the right direction.

"How about *you* go to the junkyard?" That response was always bewildering. How would I get there? How would I identify another 1986 Buick Regal in a mountain of rusted cars and twisted metal? And how would I know how to extract and then install an antenna?

They turned off the radio, and we drove in baffled silence. Music had, at one time, probably been important to both of my parents. My mother had a huge collection of 45s collecting dust in the attic. I knew my stepfather had seen Ratt once, and also had every good Aerosmith album on cassette. If our car rides had been wrought with meaningful insights to the depth of each other's character, then I would have understood. If we had driven to Sears and to the gas station choked with tears of momentous joy from the revelations being had, then perhaps we would not have had need for a working radio. Instead, there were accusations of the one who smelled it being the one who dealt it and the empty silence of four people bound by the obligations of blood and marriage. *Carly farted. She started it. Shut up, both of you.*

Occasionally, if we drove past a radio tower or, perhaps, a magnetic field, one station would come in. That station was WBLI, the worst radio station ever. Its format was, and still is, awful pop songs for divorced moms to jam to. Carly and I became experts at changing lyrics on the fly, a skill that has carried over into my adulthood. As a dog owner, I have discovered that the word "love" is easily replaced in any song with "pug" for an instant hit, as in "What's Pug Got to Do With It?" or "Ain't Talking 'Bout Pug." Tina Turner and David Lee Roth can eat their hearts out, because with a radio and a small dog to dance with, I am an unstoppable hurricane of rock and roll.

Even after I started to buy CDs, I still tuned in to the FM to tape songs off of the radio. I did this well into my teenage years, watching *Touched by an Angel* with my mom on Friday nights, then retreating to my room in the hopes that I might catch "Sunday Bloody Sunday" playing on WBAB. I had tons of tapes, the first five seconds of every song cut off in the scramble of stopping whatever it was I was doing to get to the record button. I gave these tapes to Carly one day in a seizure of judgment, and she taped over them with Tupac, No Doubt, and Ma$e. A sacrilege. Somewhere in the world, Bono is crying. Actually, it has been statistically proven that every thirty seconds, somewhere in the world, Bono really is crying.

My parents did not get another car until I was sixteen, deeming the Buick unsafe and allowing it to rot in the driveway on bald tires until I passed my road test. They bought a minivan, and, nearly a decade later, our prayers for a working stereo were answered. That same summer, they got us season passes to Six Flags. It was like Christmas, though the closest theme park to our area was Six Flags Great Adventure in New Jersey, which should pretty much be called Six Flags Over Hot Dogs and Gang Members.

The real cherry on the trip was that our parents gave the okay for us to go to the drive-thru safari attached to the park. Anytime we had been there on vacation, the vinyl top of the Buick as well as the many other parts that were peeling off of it prevented us from the experience of being up-close and personal with the angry, displaced creatures of the African grasslands. My sister and I were unreasonably excited about this windfall of good fortune.

"I'm totally going to keep a monkey!" said Carly. She was fourteen and had unrealistic expectations for the limitations of a drive-thru safari.

"I'm gonna touch a giraffe!" I said. There were a lot of other things I should have been hoping to touch that day. Touch a life. Touch some eyebrow wax. Touch some self-respect. However, as life and the Rolling Stones have taught me, you can't always get what you want.

We rolled through the safari park, first past ostriches and llamas and other long-necked creatures. Then rhinoceroses, elephants, hippos and other things that looked like they could really fuck up a minivan.

"Don't roll down the window!"

"Somebody farted!"

"It's just animal shit. Don't touch the window!"

"I can't breathe!"

"You're the ones who wanted this so bad!"

We went through a tall gate clearly separating whatever we were approaching from the rest of the animal population. DO NOT ROLL DOWN WINDOWS. KEEP ALL HANDS

INSIDE. RETRACT ALL CAR ANTENNAS.
"Why are there so many warning signs?" Carly asked.
"How come you're not retracting the antenna?" I asked.
"It doesn't retract," my stepfather said, shrugging.

And with that, the monkeys were upon us. The monkeys of the Six Flags Great Adventure Safari Park were unlike any other breed of monkey. They were not the Magilla Gorilla or *Dunston Checks In* I had seen on TV. These monkeys had been mutated in much the same way the men and women of New Jersey were mutated. Their fur stood on end, teased in the fashion of a groupie giving someone a handy near a dumpster outside of a Bon Jovi tribute show in Toms River. They were angry, sad, and captive like the protagonists of a Springsteen song. If we had been allowed to roll down the windows, we would have found they smelled like Suave hair products, blue-collar frustration, and hate. In the true spirit of Jersey, they leapt upon our car in a frenzy of rage.

"Don't open the windows!"
"They're trying to take off the license plate!"
"They're eating the paint off of that other car!"
"I don't want one anymore!"

Then, as if they sensed our biggest fear, one of them saw the antenna and went for it. We watched in mute terror as the monkey looked *right at us* and swung the antenna from side to side.

"Oh, God!" I cried, openly bargaining with a higher power. "No! Not now! Not after all these years! I'll give anything!"

Ordinarily I would have been embarrassed to have such a public freak-out, but at that moment, as the monkey stared at us with yellow eyes, sitting on the hood of the minivan, nibbling the end of the antenna, we were a family, and we were all in this *together*.

"Go faster!" Carly said.
"Kill them!" I found myself saying. Me. The vegetarian.
"Sonofabitch," my stepfather said. Without saying another word, he quietly navigated us through to the exit, where the monkeys were zapped by an invisible force and ran off to attack another car. There were a few scratches and a smudge of monkey shit on the roof, but we had made it through, my parents, my sister, the antenna, and I. And the hamburgers, the ten-dollar cups of soda, and even the air sucked out of our lungs on the

Freefall tasted much sweeter that afternoon on The Day We Got Attacked By Monkeys.

Growing up in Lake Ronkonkoma has taught me a lot about what it means to be truly disappointed. The trash-strewn parking lots, the seasonal homeless drifters, the syringes on the beach at the lake. But being away from it has taught me about what it means to be grateful. The five classic rock stations which may or may not be playing Twisted Sister at any given time, the record store down the street, and the family sleeping upstairs as I turn the key to come home again. I was burning to leave for so long, but it is nice to know they're here, these things I come home to, like a song I can't change the words to and probably wouldn't want to anyway.

# Peach Pits

I wasn't allowed to watch the first season of *Beverly Hills, 90210*. It's not that my parents had any opposition to child-inappropriate television viewing, as our family Saturday nights included a triple-header of *Cops*, *America's Most Wanted*, and *Tales From the Crypt*, and, therefore I had seen more sexual situations by the age of nine than I have in the last ten years of my life. It's that *90210* came on at nine and my bedtime was a modest 8:30 p.m., an unwavering fact I was sure was chiseled biblically into a stone tablet hidden somewhere towards the back of my mother's closet.

I had no real desire to see *90210*, but every Thursday morning, my third-grade class was filled in on what had happened the night before by Debbie D'Auria, who, if you hadn't seen her in the back of the classroom sitting next to a tub of broken crayons, you might have mistaken her for a tanning salon attendant, or, perhaps, a recovering junkie.

"Yo!" she said, bursting into the room and slamming her Tweety Bird backpack onto her desk. "Did anybody see 90210s last night? Dylan and Brenda was makin' out and Mr. Walsh came home- SNAP!"

I sat in front of Debbie, and though I was studious almost to the point of invisibility, I enjoyed her outbursts as a welcome break from thinking about the toothless, screaming domestic abusers I had seen on *Cops* that week. My parents watched *Cops* with such wild-eyed mania that I had begun to believe they probably recognized a bit of themselves in the amped up sex workers trying to stuff baggies of crack in their anuses in the back of the police cruiser.

The social hierarchy of Gatelot Avenue Elementary seemed to be based upon two things: 1) your sexual development. Debbie had almost certainly had her first period in utero and D-sized breasts by walking age, and for this reason, would always be top dog. And 2) whether or not your parents let you stay up on Wednesday to watch the tribulations of two beguilingly attractive fraternal twins placed in the topsy-turvy sexual playground of Southern California.

"Ma, can I stay up to watch *90210?*" It was after dinner and I was downstairs rooting through a laundry basket for a clean pair of pajamas.

"No," my mother said, certain and unyielding. Ashes fell from her cigarette and drifted onto a pile of folded towels.

"It's just that all the kids in school watch it, and I...."

"Next year. Maybe." She dismissed me with a wave of her hand. My mother was a stay-at-home mom for most of my childhood, and though she had the whole day to unwind while my sister and I were at school, the last precious hours she held dear, using them to flip between QVC and the Home Shopping Network with one hand, and with the other, pinch my stepfather's nose closed while he lay snoring in the recliner a few feet away.

"Ya too *lo-ud,*" she'd say in taunting singsong when he started to gasp for air. "I can't hear my *chan-nel.*"

Most kids would have stayed up anyway, turning on their bedroom televisions with the sound way down low. I dared not try, knowing full well my mother would sense a disturbance in the force and then we'd all end up a "Case of the Week" on *America's Most Wanted.*

It never occurred to me to go against any of my parents' rules. They were like wild animals and I regarded them with the careful vigilance and guarded curiosity that a zookeeper might afford a bobcat or cougar. In their habitats, they were terrifying and beautiful: my mother, filing her nails with her cubic zirconia rings shining in the blue light of the television, and my stepfather, sleeping without a shirt, mouth agape, lightly drooling. From a distance, they were magnificent. If provoked, their chest-beating could shake the leaves from the palm fronds, or, more accurately, the picture frames from the top of the VCR.

When the new school year rolled around, I was finally allowed to stay up late enough for *90210.* My younger sister, Carly, was also allowed to stay up, which I felt was cheating, because she should also have to suffer for a year as I had done. My parents were more lenient on Carly with nearly everything, though they would never admit to it. I needed to employ a spectrum of tactics from bribery to logic-based pie charts and histograms to do nearly anything. I had to practically run a gauntlet of fire and broken glass to ride my bike to the candy store, but Carly just ran there and nobody seemed to notice.

I greatly resented both Carly and my parents for this oversight of judgment, but once we were all sitting down and the saxophone- heavy theme music began to play, my animosity disappeared and I was transported. I was no longer a nine year old sitting Indian-style in a smoky, wood-paneled living room, but a glamorous teenager feeling her wild oats in the Hollywood jungle. My favorite character by far was Jason Priestley's Brandon Walsh. He worked for the school newspaper, drove a copper Chevette, and dared to rock a feathered, corn silk, post-Swayze mullet in the early 90s. He was a dreamboat, and I wanted to be the skipper. Knowing what I now know about myself, I'm not so sure I had a crush on him so much as I wanted to *be him*. Carly took a shining to Luke Perry's character, but Dylan was a little too brooding for me. Brandon was cavalier without being too cool. It was a thin line, but he straddled it, in tight Gitano jeans. Debbie D'Auria was no longer in my class to hear her play-by-play of the episode I had seen, but I imagined what our conversation would be as I lay in my bed that night, too excited for sleep.

*"Yo!" Debbie announces herself, sliding into the classroom on a greased pole. "Anybody see 90210s last night?"*

*The room is silent, that is until I rise from my desk, sporting a blonde side-ponytail and a black sequined evening gown. "I did," I say, raising a satin glove, "and it was totally boss to the max."*

*Then my entire fourth grade class hops in my Chevelle to go get burgers at the local hangout run by a friendly trusted adult-slash-confidante.*

In short order, Carly and I became super-fans. We had dolls, posters, and oversized T-shirts with the whole cast on them that we wore for sweet dreams. *90210* began to warp any notion I had of what it meant to be a teenager. I knew we were poor, but if I could just get my stepfather's entire asphalt worker's union transferred and all of my mother's porcelain dolls and sapphire pendants rerouted from the Home Shopping Network to Beverly Hills, everything would be alright. The Walsh family had moved from Minnesota, which my rudimentary knowledge of geography told me was probably a lot like Long Island. I was sure they just edited out the parts where the mom bought As Seen On TV products on credit and the dad threatened to fill the pool with dirt if everybody didn't shut up. They couldn't have been much better off than we were.

"If yous like the show so much, why doncha write them a letter?" My mother was running on the new treadmill, watching local crime reports on TV with a lit cigarette resting where a water bottle was supposed to go near the control panel.

The idea was preposterous. *Us* write *them* a letter? That was like asking us to call the President. Yeah, ma. I'll just get him on the horn. Why don't I reach up and pull a star from the sky while I'm at it? Because you're living in a fantasyland, woman. *I could never write Jason Priestley a letter.*

Besides, we probably didn't have any paper or sharp pencils.

When she was done running, my mother found an old notebook and excavated two pens from a junk drawer.

Now we really had no excuse. How could I, in my unsophisticated fourth grade ineloquence, possibly sum up all the deep feelings I had for Jason Priestly? If D.H. Lawrence had been lucky enough to catch even the pilot, there's no way he'd be able to express his profound gratitude and awe for such a powerful, emotionally moving character. *No way*. But here goes nothing:

*Dear Jason,*
*My name is Cassie. I watch your show all the time and definitely think you're the coolest character, way cooler than Dylan even. Anyways, if you are ever in Lake Ronkonkoma, you should come to my house. We live on Carl Street.*
*~~From~~ LOVE,*
*Cassie J. Sneider*

I finished my letter with a self-satisfied sigh. It was subtle, yet said everything I needed to say. My mom was right: what a relief.

"Hey, Carly. Can I see your letter?"

"I'm stuck," she said, thoughtfully chewing the end of a pen. Her bangs hung in her eyes and she had a look of deep concentration, as if considering a winning chess move.

"Lemme see," I said, snatching the letter. Carly had chosen to write to Tori Spelling. She was aiming low by going for the least desirable character, but it was a clever move because Tori Spelling was also the most likely character to have the free time to answer her own mail, sitting at a glass-topped table in a penthouse on Hollywood Boulevard, looking something like an upright shaved pug. She would probably send Carly a dozen roses and a plane ticket. Bitch.

*Dear Tori,*
  *My name is Carly Jane Sneider. All my friends call me Carly.*
    *From,*
    *Carly*

"Your letter is stupid," I said, handing it back with a smug superiority.

Tears formed in the corners of each eye, but Carly switched gears quickly from hurt to blind rage. She pounded the table with both fists, making a sound like the monkey in the restaurant scene in *Faces of Death*.

"What are you girls doing in there?" my mother shouted from her spot in the living room.

"Nothing! Look, Carly, you gotta say you watch the show all the time and that you think she's cool. Then she'll think you're cool, too, and then maybe she'll want to be your friend."

Carly seemed to agree with this. She crumpled up the first draft, took up a second piece of paper, and got to work with renewed fervor.

One day, nearly six months later, Carly and I were doing our homework and our mother went outside to get the mail. "Hey," she said, letting the screen door slam. "Would ya look at this!"

Jason Priestley had written me back. Not only that, but there was a *machine-printed autograph* on the postcard of him, a vision of beauty, backlit by the California sun overlooking the beaches of Santa Monica, Marina del Ray, or Van Nuys, someplace blue and wealthy looking, with a name surely more glamorous than "Patchogue Bay," "Mastic Beach," or "Robert Moses," whoever that was. This was the real deal. "All the Best, Jason Priestly."

"Whoa!" we gasped in awe.

"Don't try to touch it! You'll get your germs on it!" I cried. Carly was notoriously grubby, and the only way I was going to let her see the autograph was from behind a hermetically sealed glass case.

"Would yas shut up? Jesus Christ," my mother mumbled, opening a package of newly delivered anti-aging serum with a long, French-manicured nail.

We watched *90210* as a family for a long time. In the later years, we watched it with a sense of suspended disbelief that the entire cast would be accepted to UCLA, and later, that they would remain friends through such backstabbing and incestuous conniving. But what Carly and I couldn't have known then was that we were lucky for not having grown up in Beverly Hills. There is an appreciation one develops when Aaron Spelling is not your dad, when you grow up in a crappy place watching the local news to see if any relatives were released or indicted.

And Carly and I, if we were famous, we would answer every letter, a postcard of us walking along the brown water of Patchogue Bay, both looking down, combing the dead seaweed and trash for seashells, and a real autograph on the back.

*"We think you're cool, too. Carly and Cassie J."*

## *Sugar, Sugar*

A quick inspection of my parents' attic will reveal the psychological differences between my sister and me. One need only open up a large Tupperware bin to find my collection of My Little Ponies in immaculate condition, spit-shined by their obsessive-compulsive owner twenty years ago. Their hair has not been combed into a balding clog of synthetic yellow knots like the ponies in the bin next to it, the one covered in peeling stickers with "CARLY" written a hundred times on the outside in crayon. My ponies' hair was conditioned in the bathroom sink while I hummed Elton John songs to myself. I spoke to them. I petted them. And I still believe that this love would spur them to come to my rescue if I ever needed them.

"*Ponies! Help!*" *I say, as a flash flood rips through my childhood home.*

"*Quickly!*" *neighs Buttercup, who bites down gently on the mane of Sunshine Clover, forming a lifebridge of childhood wishes to save me from instant death.*

"*I'm drowning!*" *Carly screams, frantically clawing and trying to grab hold of anything floating by.*

"*Fuck you!*" *says Starshine, who is partially melted to Skippity Doo and mummified in peanut butter.*

Early on, Carly displayed a devil-may-care attitude toward taking care of toys, completing science projects, and brushing her hair. Despite our many differences, Carly and I banded together every Halloween. I didn't have any other friends to go trick or treating with, and I think my mother was under the assumption that I would be able to defend the two of us against teenagers with shaving cream.

We didn't have much money, so when Halloween rolled around, our mom usually brought us to Woolworth's to scrounge for deals like raccoons tipping over a trashcan. Carly was a happy-go-lucky eight year-old and didn't mind when the only choice she was presented with was Witch or Ghost. I, on the other hand, was ten and therefore old enough to feel weirded-out that the only costume left in my size was a sexy wizard outfit.

"But I don't want to be a wizard," I said, looking at the valley of implanted cleavage on the package. The wizard model had classic early 90s features that suggested a potential career in Cinemax soft core: rigid, oversized breasts, bleached hair, and Wet 'n' Wild lip liner in 'Bus Stop Skank Brown.'

"Tough. It's the day before Halloween," my mother said, filling out the check and handing it to the cashier.

"But it's October. I'm gonna be cold." The lady on the package was wearing fishnets, and I was sure that they would do little to insulate against the fall chill.

"Wear pants underneath it. Let's go," she said, digging the keys out of her pocketbook.

The next day when I was wearing white stretch pants and a turtleneck under my sexy wizard costume, I felt cheated. I understood that I was only in the fourth grade, but I had hoped that when I put on the pointy blue lamé hat, a transformation would take place. Maybe I could use the felt wand it came with to amaze the neighbors by beaming candy into my bag, or to deflect the psychotic teenagers in my neighborhood when they inevitably tried to egg us.

"You don't look like the box," Carly said, waving around her arms in an attempt to haunt the bathroom where I stood looking in the mirror. I stared at my reflection, seeing my Tom McCann sneakers and the sweater bunching out of the plunging neckline. I stared and I squinted, and, finally, I let it sink in that I was, despite my best efforts, a total gaylord.

"Girls! Get downstairs! Your cousins are here!"

Lisa and Wendy were even poorer than we were. This was evident by the witch hats they were both sporting in addition to jack-o-lantern boxers on the outside of their clothes. My cousin Jamie was dressed as a devil. This was fitting, because Jamie's room was a hell-on-earth for toys. When the neck on my favorite Barbie snapped, we went to my aunt's house to dig through the headless, undressed graveyard in Jamie's closet.

"Here. Take this one," Jamie had said, ripping the head off of Ice Capades Barbie with a remorseless pop.

We gathered in our dining room, a ragtag band of discount spooks and bargain frightmares. When my mother handed out sacks for our loot I begged for the pillowcase from my father's bachelor days with the pair of enormous breasts silk-screened on it. I was rebuked with a stern glare. Instead I got an orange and brown one from the back of the closet that smelled like dust mites and Watergate.

"Have fun!" said my aunt.

"We used to put pennies in socks and swing them around," my mother said and she pushed us out the door.

Halloween 1993. The teenagers in the neighborhood are fueled by nad-pumping grunge music and Headbangers Ball. They walk around without costumes, their hair sprayed green and pink, or if their parents don't care about them, it is dyed in shades of fading Kool Aid. They roll in groups of anywhere from two to twelve, spraying parked cars with silly string, egging the houses that turn off their lights and pretend not to be home.

Nothing is sacred.

I am walking with my cousins. I am aware of the crunching of leaves under my feet, of the cold stinging everywhere the turtleneck and sexy wizard costume do not conceal. Carly is making ghost noises, Jamie and Wendy are swinging pillowcases at each other, and Lisa is talking about someone in her homeroom named Jarrod whom she is interested in marrying. She has decided that the bridesmaid colors will either be burgundy or hunter green, and their firstborn child will probably be a girl.

We are walking together but it feels like a solo mission. I have left the relative safety of my home to collect as much candy as possible. Once I return home, my objective will then switch to protecting the good candy from my parents, who are shameless scavengers and will claim all the Almond Joys have poison in them. We walk for blocks. Old people meet us at their gates and cast pennies into our sacks. Pennies mean they do not ever leave their house. They smile at our costumes as if they have never seen a devil or witch or ghost before. No one seems to notice my ill-fitting sexy wizard. I accept their pennies, which are worthless, and say nothing.

Our neighborhood does not have sidewalks, and we trudge on through piles of wet leaves. The bottom of Carly's ghost costume begins to brown, and I have somehow gotten a smear of mud on my sexy wizardry, making it seem as though I have had a magic spell of incontinence. Minivans fly past us, piloted by parents who understand that trick or treating is a game of speed as well as deft politeness. If they are careful, their children will have candy to hold them over until Easter. Trick or treating by foot is difficult, but it is boot camp preparation for real life, for situations such as walking to work after a succession of failed DMV tests and running to class after the car stalls in the university parking lot. I will not have candy until spring, but I will be a better person in the springtime of my life.

We approached a run-down house with no decorations and knocked on the door. After a few minutes of patient waiting, an old man came to the door with a basket of Mary Janes and Bit-o-Honeys, which are the equivalent of pennies for the elderly who are still mobile.

"Oh!" he said, in the delighted way old people do when they are genuinely glad to answer the door to something other than a reaper holding a scythe with their name on it.

Lisa, Wendy, and I lined up and he dropped a few orange and black nuggets into our sacks. The old man stepped back and took a long look at Carly and Jamie.

"Ooooh! WooOOOoo!" Carly said, waving her white polyester fringe arms and holding open her pillowcase in anticipation.

"Youse two was here already!" the old man proclaimed and slammed the door shut in their smiling faces.

We stood in the yard outside of his house, dumbfounded by the coldness of his denial. The fact was that we had not been to his house at all that day. He clearly had a basket of shitty candy for the taking, and most adults, even if they felt they were being swindled, would begrudgingly accept the loss in the name of goodwill.

"What a *dick!*" Jamie said. She was a year older than me and was allowed to say words like "dick" and "hell."

"We oughtta tell Ma!" Carly said, eyes welling up with tears. She was only eight but could still recognize that our mother was mildly psychotic and might be willing to kill that old man if she knew we'd been smited.

"We could put poop in a bag and leave it on his doorstep!" I suggested, vengeful even as a fourth grader.

It was getting dark. We made the walk back to our house thinking of the millions of ways we could torment our eighty year-old neighbor. Most of the ideas we came up with involved eggs, shaving cream, or the harvesting of dog poop. In the end, we did nothing, but if you ask Carly or Jamie about that old man today, they will respond with an anger so venomous that one would think the incident had happened yesterday.

Our cousins went home, and Carly and I began the intense negotiations of trading candy. I arranged mine into piles of universally recognized value based on sugar content and rarity. Carly dumped hers in a pile on the floor and took anything in danger of being eaten by our parents upstairs to bury in a hollow spot she had made in the box spring of our bunk beds. Sometimes, I would wake up in the middle of the night to hear her sucking on a jawbreaker, wrapping it up in plastic, and putting it back in the hole in the bed. It is truly a medical miracle that Carly escaped childhood without incident of worms.

Although her methods were unconventional, Carly knew what she was doing when it came to trading candy. She did not organize her pile with the obsessive pride I took great joy in. It would appear to an unskilled trader that she had no idea what she was doing, but she had a great poker face when it came to value, and she played all the good candies close to the hip. Negotiating a deal for something like a package of Twizzlers or box of Nerds could take hours or days. She would torture me with it, leaving it in plain view until the temptation got to me and I would be willing to trade anything for it. She may have been younger, but she knew what she was doing. She was cunning, shrewd and manipulative.

We fought when we were kids, but we always managed to make up before we fell asleep. A dispute over a Butterfinger was hashed out in its own way while we were in the bathroom together, brushing the sugar sweaters off of our teeth.

"Doucheburger," she said with a mouth full of toothpaste.

"Scroat," I said, spitting into the sink.

Even though I had my own room, I slept on the top bunk of Carly's bed for a long time. Our mother pried a few Smarties out of Carly's clenched fist, kissed us goodnight, and turned out the lights.

"Hey, Carlt...."

"Yeah, Cass?"

"*Youse two was here already!*" I said, and we burst out laughing.

There was a long pause. The wind outside whipped branches against the windowpanes. My stepfather snored in the next room. I heard the sound of Carly reaching around in the box spring and unwrapping a jawbreaker.

"Hey, Cass…."
"Yeah, Carlt?"
"Love you."
"Love you, too."

# Turn the Page

Go back to the places you used to frequent, go back to them and find that something is missing, something small or hard to notice, something like fresh carpet or a burnt-out neon sign. Or maybe they tore it down, maybe your favorite person, the one who kept you coming back, is suddenly gone. Maybe it just seems smaller, or maybe, just maybe, the thing that's missing is you. The Old You. The You who used to go there in the first place.

I was home on Long Island between reading tours and decided to stop by the bookstore where I used to work, which is something I never do. At this juncture in my life, I have had thirtysomething jobs, and no matter what the job entailed, it was never the normal people who came back to visit. It was the emotionally disturbed ghosts, rattling around the old haunt, asking who still worked there, stuck on this mortal plane in a developmental purgatory. It is because of these twitching, transparent spectres of retail that not visiting old jobs has become part of my psychological code. A rolling stone grows no moss, and a person who doesn't look back never becomes a lonely bag of bones, popping in to ask who the manager is. But, I was late for a birthday party and needed a card. And I just so happened to have some copies of my comic books to give away.

"How's it going?" I said to the cashier, putting my stuff on the counter. "Can you give these to Sam and Patricia?"

I worked at the bookstore for a long time, but nowhere near as long as Sam and Patricia. They had been working there for so long, it was impossible to imagine them in any other environment. Patricia, with a rattail snaking down the length of her back, gigantic cannonball-sized breasts, and shirts with wolves on them she wore without the slightest touch of ironic intent, and Sam, who had an arm that ended at the elbow and would train new employees by making them ring up copies of

*The One-Armed Chef* and the Aimee Mann album *The Forgotten Arm*. These women were the wallpaper of Borders Store #79. They were unchanging in their ways, steadfast in their work habits, and by far, the most efficient workers among us. And, I did everything in my power to wrangle an invite to hang out with them.

"Patricia," I said, twirling the rattail I had let a friend chop into my hair. "I'm growing one, too. Now can I join your pool league?"

Patricia laughed, adjusting her mammoth bra. "Maybe," she said, and turned around to continue shelving a cart of Sue Grafton books.

We never did get to hang out, and it was years since I worked at the bookstore, but I was sure if anyone would appreciate the paper trail of toner and Xeroxed stories I was mailing across the country, it would be those women.

The cashier bagged my purchase and scanned my membership discount. "Um, the company restructured and they eliminated both of their positions. I think Sam works at a bank now. I don't know where Patricia went." I must have looked gutshot. "I'm really sorry."

It is difficult to imagine old friends in new settings. Sam sending deposit slips along in a vacuum tube at the teller window of the Credit Union, or Patricia in anything other than a T-shirt bearing the words "New Mexico" and a pair of stained jeans. There is an alternate reality where they move on without you, realize their true potential, and find a happiness that doesn't involve the monotony of sorting true crime novels. Maybe they never imagined me with my shit together, remembering a family member's birthday, or at least, with a normal haircut.

But, what do I know? I'm just a ghost.

Dave worked at Barnes & Noble, and I worked at Borders.

"It's like we're Spy vs. Spy," he whispered, his voice muffled so as not to wake his parents in the next room.

"I know," I said, sitting in the living room of my parents' house in flannel pajamas and Dave's *Gimme Shelter* shirt. "Tell me your secrets. Join our side."

Our relationship lasted three years, which, for me, was my

whole life, an eternity in a time capsule of angry young freedom and the feeling of college being a relentless labyrinth of failure. Both of us lived at home, and both of us were light-years away from graduation being even a distant possibility. So, instead, we made each other laugh until our ribs felt broken and late for class so often I was on academic warning three times.

Before Dave landed the job at Barnes & Noble, he worked at Tower Records with the rest of our friends. The dress code there was somewhere in the range of laissez-faire to obscene. It wasn't uncommon to see Cradle of Filth shirts with crucified animals or naked women, the uncensored wardrobe of true liberty, coming in increments of $5.35 an hour. When Dave started at Barnes & Noble, he was stressed because his only work-appropriate shirt with a collar had a cigarette burn in the pocket. I, on the other hand, had no dress code to abide by, although I had recently gotten in trouble for wearing a pair of child's gun holsters from the 1950s to work. If how you dress for your job provides the basis for the way people see you, then I was an eagle flying boldly over the Rockies, a gunslinger, unbound by the obligations of collars or pleated pants.

"Barnes & Noble is just more sophisticated," he said. "We wear nice clothing so that our clientele will respect our choices."

"Screw your clientele," I said. "The degenerates that come into Borders love us because we're diverse."

That was my argument. Barnes & Noble employees were like pleated khakis neatly folded into the drawer of someone on ten different kinds of anti-psychotic meds. But Borders employees were the anti-psychotic meds, pills and tablets of many different colors, all with unique and very important purposes. Dave and I never tired of putting down each other's employer, but none of it mattered much anyway. It was the customers we agreed we hated.

"Somebody crapped in front of the water fountain today," I said, whispering into the phone on my break. "Who does that? Who?"

"At my job, they don't ever flush," said Dave on the other end of the line. "I think it's a weird attention thing. Like the way flashers just get off by you reacting. They're like animals, these people."

One of the plagues of retail is the regular customer. The only thing regular about them is that they are regularly there, messing up what you just fixed, arguing with the manager over coupons, and leering at the teenage baristas. Otherwise they are exceptionally irritating and usually extraordinarily unattractive. Fortunately for me, the only thing my store did to encourage loitering was put in a cafe. Dave's store actually hosted events, which always resulted in housebound freakazoids coming out in droves. This also caused many cell phone calls of complaint made by Dave to me from the public bathroom stall.

"There's a poetry event," Dave said quietly, his voice sapped of all patience. "This metal dude is reading sexy poems about his lazy-eyed girlfriend that obviously allude to *doing it*."

"Like how?" I asked.

"He mentioned putting his sword in her stone. It's like Iron Maiden lyrics, but horrible."

I didn't like regulars when they were an interruption to my workday, but if they were the bane of someone else's existence, then it fell into the category of "people watching" and was therefore alright. The poetry reading was only held once a month, so I had plenty of time to request the night off and leaf through anything I had that might be worth reading. I brought a few pieces with me, but settled on a short story I wrote about judging mustaches based on black and white movies I watched with my grandma. It was a surefire crowd-pleaser, and I was excited by the opportunity to take a field trip to Dave's miserable obligation. Maybe my presence alone could turn what was previously eleven steps short of an AA meeting into an inspirational scene from *Dead Poet's Society*.

"Hi, my name is Matthew. For those of you new faces joining us this evening, I'm the host of tonight's event, the monthly reading of the Queens Poetry Society." Matthew looked directly into my fresh new face when he introduced himself. He had a horseshoe of brown hair that looked like the hook end of a Velcro strip, as well as a goatee, the facial hair of choice for the recently divorced. "I'm gonna get this reading going in a minute. The sign-up sheet is being passed around, but first, Carl, did you want to say a few words?"

There were thirty chairs out for a handful of people. I chose a seat in the back row, the instinct of a wannabe bad kid. Dave was working that night, listening in spite of himself over the low feedback of the store PA. An old man stood up in front and hobbled over to the microphone. Carl looked like a live-action Montgomery Burns with the decayed purple headspot of Mikhail Gorbachev. He wore enormous glasses that magnified his eyes and a look of disgust on his face as though he was perpetually sniffing an eggy fart.

"I started this club forty years ago," he said. Then he hobbled back to his folding chair and fell asleep.

"Alright," said Matthew. "That was great, Carl. Now we're gonna have our first reader. Me. This poem is called, 'My Smiling Daughters Are Like My Grandmother's Hands.'"

I didn't really understand the comparison, but I did glean that he was, indeed, recently divorced and his daughter's smiles were all he had to keep from offing himself. When he was done, Matthew called up the first reader.

"Angelina's been coming to the poetry workshop on Wednesdays. Her poems just keep getting better by the day. Come on up, Angelina!"

Angelina was a mousey thirtysomething with huge wire-framed glasses and a frosted perm. She read with a stutter that made her difficult to understand, but "The Untouched Lotus" was clearly a poem about her sexual wish list. It was both disgusting to imagine and poorly written. I wondered if Matthew had tried to tap that, but when I looked at Dave and telepathically communicated my thoughts, he shook his head a solemn negative. I looked around at the crowd. There was Carl, our ancient founder, slumped over and possibly dead, another old man with a white mustache and a ponytail, Metal Dude and the damsel in optometry distress, two middle-aged women, a teenage girl, and me. I closed my eyes and thought about starting a band with all of them. Sort of a Polyphonic Spree meets the Kids of Whitney High. I would sing. Metal Dude would shred on bass. Carl would robot in one of those light-up jumpsuits that Daft Punk wears. Then we'd all climb in the tour bus, do lines of blow, and roll on to the next city like a Bob Seger song.

"Okay, next up we've got one of our new faces this evening. Cassie, come on down."

I shuffled my papers, still thinking about the Partridge Family I wanted to be a part of, and walked to the podium.

"Uh, hey. I'm Cassie. This is a story about mustaches."

I was in the presence of three mustaches, four if you count the middle-aged woman who was between waxes. The story went over as I thought it would, with chuckles where there should be chuckles and sighs were there should be sighs. They applauded and I took my seat.

"Wow!" said Matthew. "That was really great. We don't often get short stories up here, but that was something else. Thank you. Alright." I felt like my mission had been successfully completed. Our host looked down at the sign-up sheet. "Okay, next we've got Ned Diller. Ned, if you want to take the podium."

The old man with the white, straggly beatnik ponytail got up from his chair. Ned Diller was probably about seventy-five years old. He had the kind of mustache that you could tell he had been growing since day one of puberty, the kind that would make your kids cry if you ever shaved it because Daddy's face looks weird. He wasn't feeble like Carl, who had one hand gripping the arm of the Angel of Death just to stand upright. Ned Diller walked to the podium confident and poised, but grabbed the microphone by cupping it like it contained lightning bugs and sending a shriek of feedback throughout the store.

"Poetry *indeed*," he began, glaring at me like I was in a police line up for snatching his purse. "The *poem* I am reading today is a winter *poem*. It's called, 'White Frost on Tree Branches.'"

I was hoping for some finger-snapping or Ginsburg, but Ned's poem was the saccharine imagery of a nursing home Christmas card. It was the sort of thing you would expect from someone his age, but certainly not from someone his age *with a ponytail*.

"Thanks, Ned. That was great. Well, if none of you have anything else to read, I guess we can wrap it up. Thanks for coming out this evening. Next month's meeting will be, as always, first Monday of the month. Workshop on Wednesdays. See you all then!"

With the meeting adjourned, I walked off to go find Dave to give him my review of the evening's events and see if he wanted to get dinner. I was looking down the romance aisle when somebody punched me hard in the arm. Instinctively, I spun around with my fist clenched, ready to knock out whoever had hit me. Surprisingly, I found myself face to face with Ned Diller.

"Was that a *poem?*" he asked, wily brows knitted in anger.

"*What?*" This really caught me off guard. By that time in my life, I had been in several fistfights, but never, until that point, had I thought about striking someone so elderly.

"I *said* was that a *poem?*"

"Uh, I dunno. I guess it was sort of a poetic essay."

"I SAID," said Ned Diller, wringing his papery hands, "was that a *POEM?*"

"No," I said. "It wasn't."

"Well, young lady, this is a *POETRY* reading."

That was enough. I barely had the patience to deal with the contentious regulars at my own job, let alone in my leisure time at other people's jobs. "Oh, I'm *sorry.* Are you the Poetry Police?"

Ned's face purpled with anger. "I'm not saying I'm the Poetry Police. I'm saying that this is a *poetry* reading and it should stay that way."

"Oh, well then, why don't you arrest me, Poetry Police?" I held out my wrists limply, begging his arrest.

"In my day, young women had respect for their elders!"

"Well, in my day, old men kept their opinions to themselves!"

"Good DAY, Young Lady!"

"Good NIGHT, Old Man!"

Ned stormed through the cooking aisle and back up the escalator. I turned around and Dave was looking over a bay of romance shelves.

"Did I just hear you ask him if he was the Poetry Police?"

I had a month to prepare for the next reading. I wrote a poem I was sure was perfect, the ultimate slam, an in-your-face diss to the senior citizen who had punched me in the arm.

"You're really getting way *too* into this," Dave said. "Maybe you should do your statistics homework instead."

"No, Dave," I said, sitting with my feet on my parents' coffee table. "There is no statistics homework in *war.*"

Four weeks later, the day of reckoning was upon us, but Ned Diller wasn't there. Angelina read something pathetic and sexual. An old woman read a poem about leaves. Matthew read something about when he met his wife. I waited, a predator, a snake in the grass among the empty chairs in the basement level of Barnes & Noble. I looked to Dave where he stood at the music counter, shaking his head at me, and then to the escalator. Ned Diller rode down, confident, regal, self-assured in a way that someone who thinks winter frost makes for a good poem *should not be.*

"I've been waiting all month for this," he said. Then he handed me a paper and took a seat.

It was a Peanuts comic about a disagreement between Charlie Brown and Snoopy. He had scanned it into Microsoft Paint and put word bubbles over the dialogue to where Snoopy was now shouting, "POETRY POLICE!" The back said:

*"I have been asked to read at many different venues and had my plays put on by community theatre groups, but never in all my years of writing have I been so insulted as when the angry young lady at the Queens Poetry Society meeting had the nerve to call me the Poetry Police when I made a friendly suggestion."* Ned Diller. Copyright 2005.

I looked up. Was that all he had?

"Oh, great!" Matthew said, looking down at the list. "Next up we have Cassie. She's a real sparkplug, and I hope she becomes one of our regulars. Come on up, Cassie."

I took the podium and looked to Dave. He was still shaking his head. I breathed deeply and began my poem, a scathing four-pager about Ned Diller's funeral, written in the alternate universe where he suffered cardiac arrest after lecturing me from his expert opinion what a poem should be.

When I finished, I looked up. Dave's mouth had formed an O-ring of horror. Carl actually woke up for my reading and elbowed Ned, and Ned, well, he just looked the same. Hateful. Smug. But I sensed that he might be a little wounded on the inside.

"Well," said Matthew. "Thank you, Cassie. I think we all really needed that. Well, I guess that's about all we have time for this week. Thanks to everyone for coming down. Same time, same place next month."

And so it went. My desire to bombard myself with bad poetry eventually ran its course, and, I guess Dave and I did too. There is also a suspension of principles that has to take place in order to become a regular when you hate that sort of thing. I decided I was into being irregular, spontaneous, on-the-go. But last spring, I happened to be home on the first Monday of the month and suspended my principles long enough to end up in the basement of the Barnes & Noble in Queens.

"Ned is gonna start off this evening for us," said Matthew, handing over the microphone.

Ned, as old as he was, you could still tell he was mean. He was a little weaker, but his ponytail was still as sleek as I'm sure Seabiscuit looked in his heyday.

He put on his reading glasses. "This poem," he began, "is called 'The Empty Chair.'"

It was the same boring, every-last-word-rhymes-fare I was used to from Ned. Then I noticed that Carl wasn't there, holding it down for the land of nod in the front row.

*Oh, God. Not Carl.*

"Thank you, Ned. That was beautiful. Our next reader, well, some people are like favorite songs. You think about them sometimes and then they come on the radio and it just brightens your day. Cassie is one of those readers. What do you have to share with us tonight, Cassie?"

Matthew was right. People are like songs on the radio, playing somewhere invisibly when you are not around on a wavelength you can't hear. Then, one day if you are lucky, you tune in at the right moment and hear them for one last time.

"Haven't seen you in a while," Ned said, shaking my hand.

"Haven't seen you either."

4:20
Saturday

This is a polite but heartfelt request to please turn ~~off~~ the music down to a background level. I drove all the way across town to pick out a new book. I can't even read ~~a sentence~~ without the interference of some 70's vocals. This is not a nightclub. It's a bookstore.

Caroline ▮▮▮
584 - ▮▮▮▮

## *Mole*

The headlights of the cars drove on an invisible track across the ceiling and I was lying in my mother's bed. A T-shirt that didn't smell like my dad anymore slept peacefully between us, not knowing it was only enjoying the comfort of a bed because it was being used for its smell. The T-shirt didn't know he was gone yet, and I wondered if the half-smoked cigarette in the ashtray next to my side of the bed knew its last drag would never be tasted. I was five years-old and wide awake, wondering if the cars were projecting themselves onto the ceiling so I could think about them, instead of how I was lying in the empty space of someone I knew was never coming back.

My uncle had died before I was born, overdosing on heroin, and leaving his twin and my father to take care of everything he'd left behind, which included a pregnant girlfriend, a wreck of an apartment, and a closet full of personal effects. My father sorted through the papers and overdue bills while my other uncle sat on the bed trying on a pair of boots.

"What the hell are you doing?" my father asked.

"These are perfectly good boots," he said, knotting the laces.

"They're *a dead man's* boots!" my father said.

"They're *perfectly good* boots," my uncle corrected, and he took them home.

I was with my dad when they broke the news. We drove from doctor to doctor that day, white knuckles on the steering wheel of the pickup truck. When we got home he told my mother, and everything after that was a blur, mental pictures ripped up and thrown out; faces scratched and negatives burnt. The day he left for the hospital, we sat on the bed and he pulled up his socks over gray feet, the feet of someone with a heart older than their thirty-two years.

"Buddy, I need you to tell Uncle George something."

"What, Daddy?"

"I want you to tell Uncle George to stay the hell away from my shoes."

"That's a curse." I was well-trained.

"You can say it just this once."

I don't remember seeing my dad in the hospital. I don't remember seeing him on morphine, or my mother walking in on him sitting up in the crisp, white bed, pretending to sew.

"Keith, what are you doing?"

"I'm sewing wings," he said with his eyes closed, thumb and forefinger making sweeping circles in the air.

I do remember wondering what "intensive care" was. I remember wishing my dad had a dictionary in his dresser instead of a 1980 edition of the *Guinness Book of World Records* so I could learn what the words meant. I remember spending a lot of time at my aunt's house, in the sprinkler, in the sun. I remember listening to my dad.

"Uncle George," I said, nervous about using the H word. "Daddy said to stay the hell away from his shoes." My mother and uncle went pale. Exeunt. Fin. Fade to black.

I hated the dark. The bedrooms of our house were permanently bathed in streetlight. A fuzzy dark orange fell on my mother's face. She hadn't been sleeping and I had a sore throat again. I had climbed into my dad's spot next to the shirt to count the cars. With the looming prospect of having my tonsils taken out and no dictionary to tell me what they were, I needed something more real than sheep.

"Do you know how to pray?" my mother asked after she'd turned off the lights.

The only thing I knew about God was the tattoo of Jesus on my dad's arm, and that he said he was an atheist. My reply came in the form of a vigorous headshake.

"You put your hands together like this. Then you say *ourfatherwhoartinheavenhallowedbethyname*. Then you can talk to Daddy if you want." She turned over and I was left to try to remember all those words, hallowed in thy name. They didn't mean anything to me, but did they open a porthole, a skipped stitch in the space-time continuum, that allowed the living to speak to the dead and the dead to hear them in their graves?

Was that what it was?

"Um, today in school Miss Welch yelled at me because I went to the school store to get a pencil and when I got back she was already teaching."

*From within the pine of his coffin, my father makes a fist. If radiation should leak into the ground and all the dead fathers of all the five year-olds should rise as a collective body, the first thing they will do is shuffle to the local elementary school and eat the brains of every Kindergarten teacher. Then they will go to the Home Depot and look at tools. My father will test-drive a riding lawn mower. Then they will look at their watches and return to their graves in a punctual and orderly fashion.*

When I was six, I was forced into the World of Girl Scouting, which in hindsight is as corrupt as the World of Mail-Order Brides or the World of Swallowing Balloons of Cocaine and Smuggling Them Across the Border. Girl Scouting is a form of trickle-down capitalism, the troop leaders shrewd and cunning businesswomen, and the Scouts proletarian worker bees, our tiny hands being frostbitten in subzero weather to push our product. For every box of Tagalongs, three Girl Scouts are sold on the black market. For each package of Samoas, one Girl Scout is put to death. The statistics are as chilling as a bite of a Thin Mint.

The lessons we learned as Scouts were nothing short of useless.

"Today we're going to learn about nutrition!" said Miss Leeann, our troop leader.

Everyone cheered. I silently picked a scab.

Miss Leeann produced a piece of loose-leaf paper, a carrot, and a jar of mayonnaise. "When something has fat in it, and you rub it on paper, the paper will magically turn clear." She spooned a glob of mayonnaise onto the paper. The troop watched with bated breath. Miss Leeann wiped the mayonnaise off the loose-leaf and held it up for all to see. "The mayonnaise left a clear spot. That means it's bad for you."

The troop booed the mayonnaise. I, on the other hand, was mayonnaise's biggest proponent. Every day for lunch, I asked for mayonnaise on white bread, and every day I was told by my mother that everyone would think I was on welfare. The way she pronounced "welfare" made me think that being on it was like accidentally stepping in crap. Welfare was nothing that couldn't be scraped off onto a lawn or doormat, and I proudly ate my mayonnaise.

Miss Leeann brandished the carrot and crumbled the loose-leaf tainted by the fatty mayonnaise. She rubbed the carrot and held up the paper. "Carrots are good for you, because they don't leave a mark."

The troop cheered the carrot.

I kept working on my scab, and left the oohing-aaahing sheep to their loose-leaf paper.

The only thing I looked forward to in Girl Scouts was the Wish Circle. At the end of the meeting, I stood in a circle with my comrades, holding their hands while I thought of who I had seen with their fingers buried deep in their noses. Miss Leeann started us off by making a wish and squeezing the hand next to her, and we all did the same until our wishes came full circle.

I took the business of wishing very seriously. While everyone else in my troop was probably wishing for a new Popple, I was carefully considering if my wish would be twisted into a horrible monkey's paw situation that I would have to spend the rest of my life trying to rectify. The only thing I wanted was to have my father back. If I wished for him to be alive again, would I come home to him sitting in a lawn chair, partially decomposed, trying to light a cigarette? What if he needed to feast on the flesh of the living to stay alive? There were only so many scouts I could lure home without someone noticing.

For this reason I made sure to word my wish with the utmost caution:

*"I wish for everything to be exactly the way it used to be."*

One day, this wish would make my life play like a country song on rewind. I would emerge from the fluorescent basement meeting place into the warm sun and return home and me and my dad would sit on the couch watching a nature special and eating all the mayonnaise in the world.

This wish was foolproof. Even if it set time itself back to zero, I could still do it all over again. My first words would be "Watch your cholesterol!" and "Chest X-ray!"

"Did she just say chest X-ray?" my dad would say.

"I think so," my mother would say, "and she's pointing at you."

Every week, I would leave the fluorescent basement meeting place, and every week my unsinkable faith in wishes would tell me maybe next week. My mother picked me up from Girl Scouts one of those weeks. "When you do the wish circle at the end, what do you wish for?" she asked, fumbling for a cigarette with her keys in her hand.

"*Say Popples!*" said the part of my brain that was deeply embarrassed by wishing for the impossible.

I stuttered and tried to form the word Popple.

She stopped and looked through me. I watched the unlit cigarette moving up and down with her words: "If you're wishing for your father to come back, you can stop wishing because it's never going to happen."

The T-shirts were starting to smell more like an empty bed than my dad. My mother fell into a restless sleep each night with a prayer taking the place of a cigarette on her lips. I slept in my own bed, the soft orange glow falling onto my toys. God sat outside atop a wishless star, shining headlights onto my ceiling.

## *One in a Million*

I don't know if it's normal to be fully aware of every establishment open 24 hours within a fifty mile radius of my hometown, or that I go to those places by myself in an automatic response to feeling tired. I yawn once and suddenly, I am in Pathmark, admiring the selection of sticky hands in the vending machine. My friends are asleep in their beds, brushing their teeth, laying wedding rings in the soap dish. They are spooning or being spooned. I am listening to *Ga Ga Ga Ga Ga* and driving to the diner where the night manager apologizes because there is a woman in my usual booth. This woman is very overweight, and wearing culottes and sandals. I note that she is missing a toenail when I look down to scowl, seeing she is not using the one free outlet under the booth. She is eating by herself, and so am I. I sit somewhere else and order tea.

The seat will be warm when she gets up.

I am aware of the other people in the diner, of the slow, sad Sheryl Crow song playing somewhere on hidden speakers, incongruous to the erratic joyful movements of Chuck Woolery emceeing the game show on the overhead TV. He looks the same as when he hosted *Love Connection* twenty years ago, no wrinkles and a smile like he's trapped in ice, chattering. I am ten inches taller than I was twenty years ago. I don't wear sweatpants anymore. I still do not have tonsils, and I still go to bed too caffeinated for unconsciousness.

When I had my tonsils out, the anesthesiologist told me in a soothing voice that I would fall right to sleep once I breathed deeply into the mask of sweet air.

"Good luck," I said, confidently. "I don't even sleep at home."

I was out by a count of ten, and the doctor had a story for my mom when they wheeled me into the recovery room.

I was being truthful to the anesthesiologist, breaking it down for him, letting him know I was a six year-old insomniac.

I didn't, until now, think about the amount of soda we drank as a family, liter upon liter at every meal. We were a Pepsi household, firmly patriotic in our dedication. To drink anything else went against an unspoken rule of what it was that Sneiders did and did not do. My father was very clear about these things while he was alive. Sneiders hung toilet paper like this and not like that. Sneiders did not cry. Sneiders did not get mad, they got even.

Sneiders drank Pepsi at every meal. Sneiders did not sleep. Sneiders lay in bed at night, shaking from caffeine and bolting upright in the morning, still jittery, ready to do it all over again. Ready to get even, to not cry, to hang toilet paper the right way.

My favorite relative growing up was not a Sneider, but he was close. Chris was my cousin's boyfriend. He'd been kicked out by his parents for outrunning the track coach at school while he was high, so he lived in the basement of my uncle's house. He wore shirts with skulls and band names in drippy fonts, and had giant, bloodshot eyes from sleeping even less than the rest of us. Chris had a mynah bird that he kept next to a microwave, and the only sound it learned to make was the beep signifying time was up on reheated pizza and store-brand Pop-Tarts. The bird rang at all hours of the night, never sleeping, replicating in perfect pitch the readiness of phantom popcorn and non-existent TV dinners. Chris could not release the bird into the wild. Other birds would not understand it the way Marie Callender, Mrs. Fields, or any of our sleep-deprived lot could. The bird lived its life next to the microwave, listening to "Welcome to the Jungle" playing through the wall, envious.

Chris was my favorite family member because he had no concept of what it was a ten year old should or should not know. He taught me that Guns N' Roses rocked and that Sting sucked. He told me dirty jokes and limericks that rhymed with my parents' names. He told me that the singer of Aerosmith humped the microphone, and that he had seen it with his own eyes. That was almost too much, but I laughed anyway. Chris can be credited with making me pee my pants from laughter more than any other Sneider, blood-related or not.

Chris was more Sneider than all of us combined, staying up all night, listening to heavy metal with his fucked-up bird beeping endlessly that something was ready. He had it in him, the drive to be awake and ready all the time and I guess that's why he took up smoking crack. He left one day and I never saw him again. I'd like to think the bird startled him out of bed one night, in a sweat like Axl in the video for "November Rain." He took off and outran us all, no difference between us and the track coach.

*Don't you know you need some time, on your own?*

It's depressing here at the diner, writing for hours, drinking coffee until I can't remember what sleep is anymore. That the time I've spent here combines and stretches out into days or weeks and never once have I run into someone like me, sitting alone, jittery, asking for more half-and-half, taking up the only booth next to an outlet. That there is never anyone else looking into the machine with the hi-bouncing balls, feeling up their jacket pockets for a spare quarter, hopped-up, shaking slightly, a vending machine hologram of a little kid with no tonsils, trying to remember what a bird impersonating a microwave sounds like.

*Don't you know you need some time, all alone?*

The author gratefully wishes to acknowledge:

Mrs. Samuels, who told me I was going to be a writer when I was eleven.

The Dwarves, for giving me something to believe in.

The kids at the St. Francis School in Austin, Texas for believing in me.

My mom, Artic, and most of my family for their laughter and forgiveness.

The Pug, for his perseverance in the face of natural adversity.

Everyone I've ever made out with.

Michelle Tea, Beth Pickens, Ali Liebegott, and FatBobby for their support.

Thanks in advance to Ted Nugent and Steve Buscemi for wanting to hang out with me and Beth Lisick when the end of the world comes.

Without Bucky Sinister, Carly J. Sneider, and Amy Watson at 1984 Printing there would be no second edition of this book, so if you enjoyed it, thank them with donuts, kind words, or soft petting.

And thanks to my friends. There sure are a lot of you.

## *About the Author*

Cassie J. Sneider is one of my favorite people to talk about because her stories always border on the improbable. Many times I've interrupted her while she is recounting some madcap adventure, unable to suspend my disbelief, with an incredulous, "Dude, no fucking way. I don't believe you." She will then inevitably produce some piece of irrefutable evidence- a photograph of a bleach blonde woman flashing a group of dads at a Jones Beach concert circa 1986, a printout of an incoherent eight page break-up email, a prosthetic leg carved out of wood, a Buck Knife stolen from an enraged redneck....

If you find yourself shaking your head in disbelief, or entertaining lingering doubts as to the veracity of these tales, allow me to reassure you that while Cassie J. Sneider is not someone you may trust with the elderly or a loaded gun, you can certainly trust her as a narrator.... Yes, Lake Ronkonkoma is the land that time forgot, yes, Long Islanders talk like that, and, yes, Cassie is a bad-ass born to rock and roll.

Ali B.
Author's best friend

For friendship, fulfillment, and that loving feeling you've been longing for, please write to:

    The Cassie J. Sneider Fanclub International
    P. O. Box 2333
    Lake Ronkonkoma, New York 11779